Economy and Society
in Early Modern Europe

Economy and Society
in Early Modern Europe

Essays from *Annales*

edited by

Peter Burke

HARPER TORCHBOOKS

Harper & Row, Publishers

New York, Evanston, San Francisco, London

Contents

The essays in this volume are taken from *Annales: économies, sociétés, civilisations,* as follows:

2 Braudel (1958), p. 723ff.
3 Cipolla (1955), p. 513ff.
4 Chabert (1957), p. 269ff.
5 Verlinden *et al.* (1955), p. 173ff.
6 Hoszowski (1961), p. 441ff.
7 Małowist (1962), p. 923ff.
8 Pach (1966), p. 1212ff.
9 Ladurie (1959), p. 3ff.

One

Introduction

Peter Burke

In the last forty years, some of the most important and stimulating history in the world has been written in France. I say 'forty' years, rather than thirty or fifty, because it was forty years ago, in Strasbourg in 1929, that Lucien Febvre and Marc Bloch founded a new historical journal, *Annales d'histoire économique et sociale*. It is this journal, known since 1946 as *Annales: économies, sociétés, civilisations*, which first published all the articles that follow. The journal has become associated with a particular style of history and a particular group of historians, whose living members include Fernand Braudel, Pierre Chaunu, Pierre Goubert, and Emmanuel Le Roy Ladurie.

Febvre and Bloch founded *Annales*, as it is simpler to call it from now on, because they were dissatisfied with the way in which history was being written in France. Febvre believed that history—the discipline—had been going through a crisis since the late nineteenth century, and that the young were turning away from it to the social sciences because these subjects satisfied their 'need for reality', as he put it, while history did not. For too many historians, he thought, 'history meant learning, if not all the details, at least as many details as possible about the mission of M. de Charnacé to the courts of the North'.

Febvre was always most severe on the diplomatic historians who wrote about foreign policy without reference to the economic and social background. He would have appreciated G. M. Young's remark that such history was 'little more than the record of what one clerk said to another clerk'. But he opposed any history that was less than total.

In famous polemical book-reviews, later reprinted in a volume with the appropriate title of *Combats pour l'histoire*, he attacked Étienne Gilson and Daniel Mornet, for example, for writing history of philosophy and literary history without integrating philosophy and literature into history in general. As for economic and social history, Febvre once announced in mid-lecture that there is no such thing; there is only history—total history, the history of all human activities and their reciprocal relationships. The moral for the practising historian was that an interdisciplinary approach was needed, 'a history impatient of frontiers and compartmentalization'. 'Historians', Febvre demanded, 'become geographers. Become lawyers too. And sociologists, and psychologists.' He took his own advice to the extent of writing several books on geography. His first important work, *Philippe II et la Franche-Comté* (1912), was concerned with political, religious and social history. He treated the crisis of 1567 in Franche-Comté as the product of three conflicts: nobility versus bourgeoisie, Catholic versus Protestant, and a centralizing monarchy versus local liberties.[1]

Marc Bloch, Febvre's younger colleague at Strasbourg and co-founder of *Annales*, needs less introduction to the English public. Several of his books have been translated. Indeed, he has come to be regarded as a kind of honorary Englishman, no doubt because of his cautious, empirical approach to history, less flamboyant, rhetorical and speculative in manner than Febvre's. But like Febvre, Bloch was concerned with the reform of history. His manifesto was a lecture he gave in 1928, the year before *Annales* began, a lecture entitled 'Towards a comparative history of European societies'.[2] A characteristic piece of work, much closer to understatement than to exaggeration, this lecture argues the case for 'an improved and more general use' of the comparative method, the study of the similarities and differences between societies, whether they are close or distant in space and time, more particularly because this method may set historians on 'the road that may lead to the discovery of real causes'. Another example of Bloch's pioneering approach is his book, *Les Rois thaumaturges* (1923), which deals with the belief current in England and France from the Middle Ages to the seventeenth century that kings had the power to heal scrofula, the 'king's evil', by touching the sufferer. This was a work on the social history of ideas, and it drew inspiration from the work of Durkheim and Lévy-Bruhl on beliefs in primitive societies. Social anthropology might well have been added to the list of disciplines which Febvre told historians to take up.[3]

It was after 1929, however, that both Febvre and Bloch produced their greatest works; one wonders what influence each had on the other. Febvre moved over to the history of ideas with his book, *Le Problème de l'incroyance au XVIe siècle* (1942). This book begins by discussing the question whether Rabelais was, as Abel Lefranc once called him, an atheist, and moves on to the more general problem of the intellectual and psychological possibility of atheism at that time. In a famous section on 'the limits of unbelief in the sixteenth century', Febvre discussed what he called (in a rather Wittgensteinian phrase) the 'mental tools' (*l'outillage mental*) of the period, emphasizing its 'primitive' nature in order to argue that the sixteenth century was not yet ready for unbelief. Religion was too much bound up with everyday life to be rejected; abstract thought was hampered by the lack (in both the Latin and the French of the time) of such concepts as 'absolute', 'relative', 'abstract', 'concrete' or 'causality'; men's sense of time, space and quantity was extremely imprecise. Febvre, like Bloch, had clearly learned from Lévy-Bruhl's book, *The Primitive Mind*. But he pushes further into historical psychology, discussing, for example, the relative importance of the five senses in the sixteenth century, and arguing (twenty years before McLuhan) that the rise of printing meant the rise of the eye.[4]

Meanwhile Marc Bloch was writing his *French Rural History* (1931), and his *Feudal Society* (1939–40), an essay in total history which moves from systems of land tenure to modes of feeling and thought.

The achievement of the founders of *Annales* has been nicely summed up by Fernand Braudel. 'Individually,' he has written, 'neither Bloch nor Febvre was the greatest historian of the time, but together both of them were.' One might add that their joint impact on the practice of history in France was even greater than their own achievements. As Braudel has put it, they established a kind of Common Market of the social sciences, 'with history as the preponderant power'. Bloch was killed by the Germans in 1944, but Febvre lived on to 1956, not only editing *Annales* but writing much of it himself, warmly encouraging the young, and scolding the others for not writing 'our' kind of history. He was nothing if not dogmatic; but perhaps one cannot make a successful revolution, intellectual any more than social, without dogmatism.[5]

Nor does one make a successful revolution without allies. Febvre and Bloch were fighting on the same side as some French social scientists with a strong interest in history, notably the geographer Vidal de la Blache and the economist Simiand.

Paul Vidal de la Blache was a generation older than Febvre, who attended his lectures at the École Normale. He was a pioneer of a new sort of geography, *la géographie humaine*, 'social geography' one might call it. He founded a new journal, the *Annales de géographie*, to spread his new conception; so even the title of *Annales* is a sort of homage to Vidal. This new geography implied 'a new conception of the relation between the land and man', as he put it. Man's relationship to the environment he saw as 'at once active and passive', shaping it and being shaped by it. Vidal's key concept was that of *genre de vie*, 'way of life', a middle term between the individual and his environment. It was this way of life (itself influenced by the environment) which decided which one of the geographical possibilities open to a society was taken up. A river might be seen by one society as a barrier, but by another as a route—it depended on their technology and their attitudes. Vidal's revolution was a 'historization' of geography, and this implied, as Febvre was perhaps the first to see, a possible and fruitful 'geographization' of history. *Genre de vie* may remind the reader of Max Weber's *Lebenstil*, 'style of life'. It seems that the *Annales* school learned from social geography what historians elsewhere, notably in the USA, have learned from sociology—to take events less seriously and structural factors more seriously than they had done.[6]

François Simiand was much the same age as Febvre, and like him a harsh critic of the traditionalist historians of the day, against whom he wrote a famous article on historical method and the social sciences, attacking three 'idols of the tribe of historians'. These were the 'idol of politics', the 'idol of the individual', and the 'idol of origins': that is, the predominance of political history over economic and social, the focusing of research on individuals rather than institutions, and the study of things when they were beginning rather than when they were important.[7]

Simiand's great positive contribution to the study of history was his work on prices. What interested him in particular were long-term trends or fluctuations. In modern history, he distinguished four periods of rising prices and production, of economic expansion, which he called 'A-phases': 1500–1650, 1789–1815, 1850–80 and 1900–20. Between these periods came 'B-phases', when prices were stable or falling, and the economy contracted. This work is interesting for several reasons. In the first place, Simiand was an economist who tried to give a *historical* explanation for the Great Slump. In the second place, he was concerned with long-term trends, rather than with the time of events. In the third place, he emphasized that price history is not a closed system, but influences, and is in turn influenced by, social and political history. As Febvre would say, there is no such thing as price history.[8]

After the Second World War, the second generation of the *Annales* school began to publish their researches. Braudel was one of the young men whom Febvre encouraged, and his book on the Mediterranean world in the age of Philip II, dedicated to Febvre, was published in 1949. The first part of the book is concerned with historical geography, 'geo-history' as he calls it, and is very much in the Vidal de la Blache and Febvre tradition. It deals with mountains and plains, with climate and communications. Braudel sees Philip II's empire above all as a 'colossal enterprise of sea and land transport', which was 'exhausted by its own size' in an age when it took a ship of fifty tons up to ten days to sail from Marseilles to Algiers. Braudel has also learned from Bloch and Simiand. The second part of his book describes price and population movements and their effects. He suggests that the Price Rise of the sixteenth century, Simiand's phase A, was favourable to very large states, like the empires of Philip II and Suleiman the Magnificent. He discusses the causes and consequences of the 'ruin of the bourgeoisie' in the Mediterranean world. Here he puts into practice his recommendation to historians (see pp. 17f. below) to take more interest in the long-term.[9]

One of the few books which can fittingly be compared with Braudel's masterpiece is Chaunu's *Séville et l'Atlantique* (1955-9). Its hero is a larger sea and the scale of the book is correspondingly more vast. The interpretative part alone, volume VIII, is over three thousand pages long. In spite of this, it is much more of a monograph and much less of a general synthesis than Braudel's book. First and foremost it is a contribution to quantitative economic history. It deals with the fluctuations in the volume of trade between Seville and the New World for a century and a half, or, more precisely, from 1504 to 1650. It turns out that there was a long phase of expansion, 1504-1622 (apart from a short-term recession in the 1550s), followed by a period of contraction; Simiand's phase A and phase B appear once more. Chaunu also argues that the economy of the whole world was becoming unified, thanks to the discovery of America, and that economic trends from Amsterdam to Peking follow the same rhythm as the trade between Seville and the New World. Chaunu is interested in structures as well as trends; in the structure of communications, for example. He makes the point that the low density of population made the New World still more vast, and that the distances were increased still further by poor communications (especially before the Spaniards came), diversity of languages as well as lack of good roads. Pizarro was able to repeat the success of Cortés ten years later because the Incas had not heard what had happened to the Aztecs.[10]

Another important work of the postwar *Annales* school is by a former pupil of Bloch's, Pierre Goubert, *Beauvais et le Beauvaisis* (1960). What Goubert originally planned to do was to write a piece of 'total history', like Bloch's *Feudal Society*, but for the Beauvais region between 1600 and 1730; 'consenting to geographical sacrifices', as Labrousse once put it, 'in order to maintain chronological ambitions'.[11] Unfortunately, the task was still too great, and Goubert decided to leave out institutions, religion (the local variety of Jansenism, for example) and social attitudes. What remains is still a remarkable work of economic and social history, a study of structure and trends (*structure, conjoncture*). There is a flourishing school of historical demography in France, with Louis Henry as its leader and *Population* as its journal. It was Henry who developed the method of 'family reconstitution', now practised by English historians like E. A. Wrigley. Goubert applied the method to the village of Auneuil. One of his achievements has been to incorporate historical demography into a more general social history. He has a long and important section on the demographic *ancien régime* in the Beauvaisis, which conformed to a Malthusian model; the population gradually rising, meeting a subsistence crisis every thirty years or so, suddenly declining, then gradually building up again. ... Another important section deals with social structure, emphasizing that the peasants of the Beauvaisis were not a homogeneous mass, but had a whole hierarchy among themselves. At the top were the prosperous ploughmen and the rent-collectors; then came the country craftsmen, the gardeners, vine-growers and bean-growers (*haricotiers*); at the bottom the agricultural labourers.[12]

The second half of Goubert's book is devoted to patterns of change. This is essentially a study of price history in the manner of Simiand and Labrousse, distinguishing short-term and long-term trends. In the long-term, he describes the fall of prices between 1647 and 1730, thus confirming Simiand's B-phase once more. Particularly interesting is Goubert's juxtaposition of price movements and population movements, showing the human consequences of economic change. When grain prices rise, as in the short-term they frequently did, population falls—the poor simply starve to death.[13]

The total history that Goubert meant to write has been triumphantly brought off by Emmanuel Le Roy Ladurie in his book *Les Paysans de Languedoc* (1966), one of the most recent and one of the most interesting works of the *Annales* school. It is not surprising that Le Roy Ladurie is sometimes referred to as the 'Dauphin'—that is, Braudel's heir to the kingdom of *Annales*. His book is concerned not only with the land, the climate (but see p. 134 below), population and prices, but also with family structure, literacy, the Reformation, peasant revolts and witchcraft. It is even more of a study of the long term than the other books I have mentioned, for it goes from the late fifteenth century to the early eighteenth, from Louis XI to Louis XIV. Such ambitions are possible, in a book of only 650 pages, because its author has restricted himself not only to one region but also to one social class. He organizes the book around economic and social change, one great movement of ebb and flow, rise and fall—Simiand's phases, but applied to total history.

In phase A, he describes a population explosion; land clearance; more intensive cultivation; a division of holdings; a price rise; and the victory of profit at the expense of rent and wages, all connected trends: an elegant demonstration of how general movements operated at the local level. But Le Roy Ladurie does not stop here. Quantitative history, though essential, is not enough. He moves on to discuss social history as contemporaries saw it and experienced it, distinguishing two cultures (one rural, Catholic, illiterate, poor; the other, urban, Calvinist, literate and prosperous) and describing peasant resentments and social conflict. He notes that in about 1580 peasant revolts in Languedoc became more radical and more violent than before; and that at the same time there was a wave of witchcraft, which he explains as a kind of escapism, a rebellion of the imagination.

From about 1650 onwards there are all the signs of a B-phase: declining population, lost villages, the reconstitution of fragmented holdings, and a drop in prices, food production and profits. Where Goubert stressed the short-term cause of population decline—starvation—Le Roy Ladurie stresses such long-term factors as emigration and later marriage. In this phase, peasant revolts take place in Protestant areas, not in Catholic ones, especially in the Cevennes. They were a response to Louis XIV's campaign against the Huguenots, for example the Revocation of the Edict of Nantes, but that is not the whole story. They are protests against taxation; but there is more to them than that. With the help of the psychologist Georges Devereux (not to mention Freud), Le Roy Ladurie offers an interpretation of the revolt of the

Camisards, in particular, with its prophets and convulsionaries, in terms of hysteria. The Camisards themselves noted that young prophetesses lost their inspiration with their virginity. The implication seems to be that even prophesying is part of phase B; declining food production leads to later marriage, later marriage to premarital sexual frustration, sexual frustration to hysteria, and hysteria to prophetic convulsions.[14]

The six historians whose work I have discussed—Febvre, Bloch, Braudel, Chaunu, Goubert and Le Roy Ladurie—are far from uniform in interests or approach to history, but they do have certain important characteristics in common. They are all very much concerned with social history. They are all interested in structural factors, the constants (at least, the relatively constant) in history, although some of them, Febvre for example, do not like the term 'structure' very much. Again, they are all interested in patterns of change, especially over the long-term, patterns which Chaunu and Goubert in particular refer to as *conjoncture*, a term taken over from the economists but now applied to total history.[15] They are not Marxists—Febvre in particular was very much opposed to any deterministic interpretation of history—but they are concerned, like Marx, with the relation between what the subtitle of *Annales* calls *économies, sociétés, civilisations*. In their conceptions of patterns of change, price and population trends are often seen as crucial factors, but the political and cultural 'superstructures' are seen as active as well as passive. For this reason the *Annales* group offers what might truly be called 'a new framework for social history'.[16] Once these points about the common characteristics of the group have been made, it is worth saying something about the differences, to see their methods as themselves changing over time between 1930 and 1970. At the present they are very much concerned with price history and historical demography, whereas neither Bloch nor Febvre was.

It must not be thought that the historians of this school are concerned only with early modern Europe, though this period has dominated their interests. They include medievalists like Jacques Le Goff and Georges Duby, and students of the nineteenth century like Charles Morazé. Nor should it be thought that social history in France is in any sense a monopoly of *Annales*. Georges Lefebvre, a contemporary of Febvre and Bloch and best known for his work on the French Revolution, was also a pioneering social historian, from the days of his book on the peasants of Northern France (1924) to that on the social structure of the Orléans area (1962). Like Febvre and Bloch, he was interested in problems of historical psychology.[17] As for other countries, there is in the USA a flourishing school of social historians who draw from (and contribute to) sociology; one thinks of historians like B. Bailyn, E. G. Barber, S. L. Thrupp, C. Tilly,[18] or of the journal *Comparative Studies in Society and History*. In England, one might say that our Febvre was R. H. Tawney (his views on the relevance of boots to economic history would have pleased Febvre); that our *Annales* is *Past and Present*; that our Chaunu or Goubert or Le Roy Ladurie is Eric Hobsbawm, Lawrence Stone or Edward Thompson. But it is more constructive to emphasize the differences between England and France. In practice, English historians take much less interest in the long-term and in total history than the French; we still have something important to learn from *Annales*.

It remains to say something about the composition of the present volume. All the articles which follow appeared in *Annales* between 1955 and 1966. They are centrally concerned with the economic and social history of early modern Europe over the long-term; hence they are introduced by a translation of Braudel's article on the long-term. Price history is represented by the next four contributions; and the remaining three articles are concerned with other sorts of history of *longue durée*.

Notes

1 See L. Febvre, *Combats pour l'histoire*, Paris, 1953, pp. 18ff., 32ff., 263ff., 284ff. Febvre's books on geography include (besides studies of Franche-Comté and the Rhine) *La Terre et l'évolution humaine*, Paris, 1922.

2 English versions in F. C. Lane and J. C. Riemersma (eds), *Enterprise and Secular Change*, London, 1953; and M. Bloch, *Land and Work in Medieval Europe*, London, 1967.

3 This book is presently being translated.

4 This book also awaits translation. There is a discussion from the social psychologist's point of view in Z. Barbu, *Problems of Historical Psychology*, London, 1960, pp. 21ff.

5 F. Braudel, article 'Febvre' in the *International Encyclopaedia of the Social Sciences*.

6 See P. Vidal de la Blache, *Tableau de la géographie de France*, Paris, 1911, and *Principes de géographie humaine*, Paris, 1921.

7 F. Simiand, 'Méthode historique et science sociale' in *Revue de synthèse historique*, 1903; reprinted in *Annales*, 1960, in homage. Compare Bloch on 'the idol of origins' in his *The Historian's Craft*, Manchester, 1954.

8 F. Simiand, *Recherches anciennes et nouvelles sur le mouvement général des prix du 16e au 19e siècle*, Paris, 1932; *Les Fluctuations économiques à longue période et la crise mondiale*, Paris, 1932. His method was applied to eighteenth-century France by E. Labrousse, *Esquisse du mouvement des prix et des revenus en France au XVIIIᵉ siècle*, Paris, 1933.

9 Braudel's *La Méditerranée*, enlarged and transformed in its second edition, is now being translated into English by Mrs S. France. There is an interesting critique of it by B. Bailyn in *Journal of Economic History*, XI, 1951.

10 For an important discussion of Chaunu's book by H. G. Koenigsberger, see the *English Historical Review*, 1961.

11 E. Labrousse *et al.*, *L'Histoire sociale, sources et méthodes*, Paris, 1967, p. 110.

12 For a summary in English, see P. Goubert, 'The French peasantry of the seventeenth century', in *Past and Present*, 1956, reprinted in T. Aston (ed.), *Crisis in Europe*, London, 1965.

13 For a summary in English see P. Goubert, 'Recent theories and research on French population between 1500 and 1700', in D. V. Glass and D. E. C. Eversley (eds), *Population in History*, London, 1965.

14 This last point is not made explicitly by the author.

15 For an example of economists' usage, see the journal *Études et conjoncture*, published by the Institut National de la Statistique et des Études économiques.

16 The phrase is J. H. Hexter's, and he has written an article with that title in *Journal of Economic History*, XV, 1955, reprinted in his *Reappraisals in History*, London, 1961. He did not, to my mind, provide such a new framework at all.

17 G. Lefebvre, *Les Paysans du Nord pendant la révolution française*, Paris, 1924; *Études orléanaises I*, Paris, 1962; *La Grande Peur de 1789*, Paris, 1932.

18 For example, B. Bailyn, *The New England Merchants in the Seventeenth Century*, Cambridge, Mass., 1955; E. G. Barber, *The Bourgeoisie in Eighteenth-century France*, Princeton, 1955; S. L. Thrupp, *The Merchant Class of Medieval London*, Ann Arbor, 1948; C. Tilly, *The Vendée*, London, 1964.

Two

History and the Social Sciences

Fernand Braudel

1 *The long-term*

The social sciences are experiencing a general crisis: they are all weighed down by their own progress, if only as a result of the accumulation of knowledge and the lack of co-operative work, while no attempt to organize the latter on intelligent lines has yet been made. Whether they like it or not, all social sciences are affected directly or indirectly by the progress of the most vigorous among them; yet they struggle on with a backward-looking, pernicious humanism that can no longer serve as a framework. All, with varying degrees of lucidity, are preoccupied with their own place in the vast body of ancient and modern discovery and this at the very time when it seems that the many paths of the social sciences must converge.

Will the social sciences meet these difficulties with further attempts at self-definition or an outburst of bad temper? Perhaps they have the illusion that these problems can be solved. Today, even more than in the recent past, and even at the risk of going back to unreal problems and arguments already dead, they are too concerned with defining their aims, methods and superiorities. We see them competing with each other, quibbling over the frontiers separating them (or not separating them adequately) from neighbouring sciences. Each one, in fact, longs to stay where it is or go back to where it once was ... Only a few isolated scholars are bringing these sciences together in a properly organized fashion: for instance, Claude Lévi-Strauss[1] is bringing 'structural' anthropology into the domain of linguistics, the horizons of 'unconscious' history and the youthful empire of 'qualitative' mathematics. His tendency is towards a science which, under the heading of 'science of communication', would connect anthropology, political economy and linguistics. But is anyone else ready to cross frontiers and regroup like this? For the sake of some petty quarrel even history and geography would break their links.

But let us not be unjust; these quarrels and refusals are of some value. The need to maintain a position against others automatically leads to fresh enquiry: to reject something implies at least acquaintance with it. Furthermore, without consciously intending to do so, social sciences cross social life in its entirety, in its 'totality'; each trespasses on its neighbours' territory while convinced that it is still on its own. Economics discovers the sociology that surrounds it; history, perhaps the least structural of all human sciences, absorbs the lessons to be learned from its proximity to so many others, and tries to reflect these lessons. Thus despite silence, opposition and indifferent ignorance, the foundations of a 'common market' are being roughly outlined; in the years to come it will be worth trying to set this common market on a firm footing, even if subsequently each science profits for a time by returning to a narrower individual path.

But the immediate need is for them to come together. In the United States this alliance has taken the form of co-operative research into the cultural regions of the modern world: 'area studies' involve first and foremost a team of 'social scientists' studying those political giants of the present day—China, India, Russia, Latin America, the United States. Getting to know these is in fact essential to our very existence. All the same, in sharing their knowledge and techniques, it is vital that the researchers do not remain wrapped up in their separate studies as was the case before, blind or deaf to what the others are saying, writing or thinking. Moreover, the unification of the social sciences must be total; the older ones should not be neglected for the sake of the more recent, which are so full of a promise that is not always fulfilled. For instance, the part allotted to geography in these American endeavours is negligible, and the role of history extremely limited. Besides, what kind of history do we mean?

The other social sciences know little of the crisis that our historical discipline has undergone during the last twenty or thirty years; they tend to misunderstand our work, and in so doing also misunderstand an aspect of social reality that history serves well but does not always make properly known—that is, social time, or those multiple and contradictory forms of time affecting the life of man, which are not only the substance of the past but also the stuff of present-day social life. In the debate that is developing between all the social sciences this is yet another cogent argument for the importance and use of history or rather of the time-dialectic exhibited in the work and sustained observation of historians. Nothing, in our opinion, comes closer to the heart of social reality than this lively, intimate, constantly recurring opposition between the instant and the long-term. Whether we are dealing with the past or present, a clear awareness of the plurality of social time is indispensable to a common methodology of the social sciences.

So I shall speak at length about history and historical time. Less for the readers of this journal,[2] who are specialists in the subject, than for our neighbours of the other social sciences: economists, physical and social anthropologists, sociologists, psychologists, linguists, demographers, geographers and even social mathematicians or statisticians— all of whom are neighbours whose experiments and research we have been following for many years now, because it seemed to us, and still does, that history in their wake, or in contact with them, is freshly illuminated. Perhaps we have something to give them in return. As a result of the recent experiments and endeavours of history, the idea of the multiplicity of time and of the exceptional value of the long-term whether conscious or not and whether accepted or not has become increasingly precise. This latter notion, far more than history itself— history with its thousand facets—ought to be of interest to our neighbours, the other social sciences.

2 History and time periods

Any historical work analyses past time and chooses between chronological systems according to more or less conscious preferences and rejections. Traditional history, giving its attention to the short-term, the individual and the event, accustomed us long ago to its sudden, dramatic, breathless narrative.

The most recent economic and social history brings cyclical oscillation into the forefront of its research and speculates on its durations: for instance it has pursued the dream, and found the reality, of the cyclical rise and fall of prices, so that there is today, alongside traditional narrative, the description of the 'conjuncture', enquiring into large sections of the past: ten-, twenty- or fifty-year periods.

Beyond this second type of narration again, there is a history of even more sustained breadth, embracing hundreds of years: it is the history of very long time periods. I learned this approach, for good or ill, when attempting to designate the opposite of what François Simiand, one of the first to follow Paul Lacombe, has christened the 'history of the event' (*l'histoire événementielle*'). The actual terms matter little; in any case our discussion will cover both poles of time, the instant and the long-term.

Not that such terms are absolutely unambiguous. For instance, 'event': personally, I should like to imprison it and restrict it to the short-term. The event is explosive, it is something new ('nouvelle sonnante', as was said in the sixteenth century). It blinds the eyes of contemporaries with clouds of smoke; but it does not endure, and its flame is hardly visible.

Philosophers would no doubt say that this deprives the word of much of its meaning. Strictly speaking, an event can acquire a whole series of references and associations. It can sometimes point to profound movements and as a result of the artificial (or genuine) game of 'cause' and 'effect', so dear to the historians of the past, it can dominate a time period far beyond its own .bounds. It can be extended to infinity and link, however loosely, a whole chain of events and underlying realities, which are thenceforth seemingly inseparable. By playing this adding game, Benedetto Croce would claim that history and man in their entirety are incorporated in every event and can, therefore, be rediscovered at will; no doubt, only if we add to the fragment something it did not contain at first glance, and therefore, only if we also know what can properly be added to it and what cannot. This difficult, dangerous game is proposed by Jean-Paul Sartre[3] in some recent reflections.

Let us try to make ourselves clearer, and speak not of 'events' but of the short-term, the tempo of individuals, of our illusions and rapid judgment—this is, above all, the chronicler's and journalist's time. Alongside great, so-called historical events, chronicles and newspapers present the ordinary accidents of life: a fire, a rail disaster, the price of wheat, a crime, a theatre production, a flood. Anyone can see that there is a short time period for all forms of life, whether economic, social, literary, institutional, religious, geographical (even a gust of wind, a storm), or political.

At first sight, the past consists of this mass of petty details, some striking, others obscure but constantly repeated; and it is they that today form the chief quarry of microsociology and sociometry—(note, too, that there is also microhistory). But this mass of detail does not constitute the whole reality of history in all its density, i.e. the material that scientific reflection can properly use. Social science virtually abhors the event. Not without reason: the short-term is the most capricious and deceptive form of time.

This, for some historians, is at the root of an intense mistrust of traditional history which may also be called the history of the event. With considerable vagueness, some confuse this label with political history, but political history is not necessarily merely the history of the event, nor condemned to be so. However, the fact is that history written in the last hundred years, almost invariably political history centring on the drama of 'great events', has been working in and on the short-term, apart only from the artificial tableaux, totally lacking in time-density ('Europe in 1500', 'the World in 1880', 'Germany on the eve of the Reformation' . . .), which it inserted in its narratives, and the lengthy explanations which were their necessary adjuncts. This was perhaps the price that had to be paid for the progress made in the same period in the acquisition of scientific tools and rigorous methods. The tremendous discovery of the document made historians think that the whole truth lay in documentary authenticity. 'It is sufficient,' Louis Halphen[4] was writing only a few years ago, 'to let oneself be, so to speak, carried along by the documents, read one after another, just as they come, in order to see the chain of events reconstituted almost of itself.' This ideal of 'history as it was born' culminated at the end of the nineteenth century in chronicles written in a new style: in their striving for precision they followed the history of events step by step just as it emerged from ambassadors' letters or parliamentary debates. But the historians of the eighteenth century and the beginning of the nineteenth century had directed their attention elsewhere—to the perspectives of the long-term, which eventually only great thinkers, such as Michelet, Ranke, Jakob Burckhardt and Fustel, were able to rediscover. If we accept the ability to go beyond the short-term as the rarest and most precious asset of the historian of the last hundred years, we shall understand the importance of the history of institutions, religions and civilizations; thanks to archaeology, which has need of vast time-scales, we shall see the pioneering role of studies devoted to classical antiquity. Not long ago they were the saving of our profession.

The recent break with the traditional forms of nineteenth-century history has not meant a total rejection of the short-term. As is well known, this break has benefited economic and social history but harmed political history. It resulted in an upheaval and an undoubted renewal; then, inevitably, came changes in method and the shifting of centres of interest, followed by the arrival of quantitative history, which is still far from exhausted.

But above all there has been a change in traditional historical time. A day or a year might seem like good units of measurement to a political historian in the past. Time was thought of as a sum of days. But a price curve, a demographic progression, the movement of wages, variations in the interest rate, the study of production (dreamed about rather than realized), any close analysis of currency, all require much larger units of measurement.

A new mode of historical narrative is emerging which we may call the 'narrative' of the 'conjuncture', the cycle or even the 'intercycle'; it offers us a choice of periods—decade, quarter-century and, at the outside, the half-century of Kondratieff's classic cycle. For instance, discounting brief, superficial accidents, prices in Europe rise between 1791 and 1817, and sink between 1817 and 1852: this slow rise and fall constitutes a complete intercycle, not simply for Europe, but, generally speaking, for the whole world. True, these chronological periods have no absolute validity. Going by other measures, such as economic growth and national income or production, François Perroux[5] proposes other limits, perhaps more valid ones; but such discussions are not important in themselves. The point is that the historian has at his disposal a new time period, taking the shape of an explanatory scheme in which history may be placed, in accordance with landmarks as yet unknown and the very pulse of the curves we have just mentioned.

Thus Ernest Labrousse and his pupils, following their manifesto at the historical congress at Rome in 1955, started work on a vast enquiry into social history, with quantification as the main centre of interest. I do not think I am betraying their secret in saying that this enquiry will inevitably result in the identification of social 'conjunctures' (and even structures), while there is nothing to assure us in advance that such conjunctures will move at the same speed as economic ones. In any case, those two important factors, economic and social conjunctures, must not make us inattentive to others whose progress is more difficult to determine and perhaps eventually will prove indeterminable for lack of any precise measure. Similarly, sciences, techniques, political institutions, mental equipment, civilizations (to use that convenient word) have all their own rhythm of life and growth, and the new conjunctural history will reach maturity only when it has perfected every part of its forces.

Logically, this type of history, by the mere fact of going beyond the short-term, should have led straight to the long-term. But, for many reasons, it has not become general practice to go beyond the short-term, and indeed a revival of the short-term is taking place before our very eyes; perhaps because it seems more necessary (or more urgent) to bind together 'cyclical' history and short-span traditional history than to press on towards the unknown. In military terms we might say it is a question of consolidating positions gained. Thus Ernest Labrousse's first important book, in 1933, studied the general movement of prices in France in the eighteenth century,[6] spanning a century or so. In 1943, in the greatest historical work to appear in France during the previous twenty-five years, this same Ernest Labrousse gave in to the need for a less cumbrous time span, when he pointed to the trough of the depression, lasting from 1774 to 1791, as itself one of the sources, one of the launching-pads, of the French revolution. Even so he was using a semi-intercycle, a large unit of measurement. His talk to the International Congress at Paris in 1948, 'How are revolutions born?', endeavours, this time, to connect economic 'pathetism' of short duration (new style) with the political 'pathetism' of the actual duration of the revolution (very old style). Here we are again in the short-term, up to our necks. Of course, the attempt is permissible and useful, but how symptomatic it is! The historian loves the role of theatrical director. How could he abandon the drama of the short-term and give up the best tricks of this age-old trade?

Beyond cycles and intercycles there is something the economists call the long-term trend—although they do not always study it. Even now it interests only a few economists, and their reflections on structural crises have not undergone the test of historical analysis, appearing as mere sketches and hypotheses rooted in the very recent past, as far back to 1929, or at the very most the 1870s.[7] However, they offer a useful introduction to long-term history. They are the first key.

The second key, a much more useful one, is the word 'structure'. For good or ill this word dominates questions involving the long-term. The word 'structure', for observers of social life, implies organization, coherence and fairly stable relationships between social realities and masses. For historians, a structure certainly means something that holds together or something that is architectural; but beyond that it means a reality which can distort the effect of time, changing its scope and speed. Certain structures live on for so long that they become stable elements for an indefinite number of generations: they encumber history, they impede and thus control its flow. Others crumble away faster. But all operate simultaneously as a support and an obstacle. As obstacles, they act as limitations ('envelopes' in the mathematical sense) from which man and his experiences can never escape. Just think of the difficulty of breaking down certain geographical frameworks, biological facts or barriers to productivity and even certain constraints of a spiritual order (mental frameworks, too, are long-term prisons).

The most readily accessible example still seems to be that of geographical constraint. For centuries man has remained the prisoner of climate, vegetation, animal population, farming potential and a slowly constructed balance from which he cannot depart without the risk of throwing everything into the melting-pot. Consider the role of the movement of flocks in mountain life, the persistence of certain forms of marine life in privileged spots on the coastline; consider the unchanging situation of towns, the continuity of roads and trade, the surprising rigidity of the geographical framework of civilization.

Similar examples of permanence and survival are to be found in the immense domain of culture. Ernst Robert Curtius's[8] magnificent book, which is at last to appear in French, is the study of a cultural system that prolongs, with changes resulting from selectivity, the Latin civilization of the Late Empire, itself weighed down under a heavy heritage: up to the thirteenth and fourteenth centuries and the birth of national literatures, the civilization of intellectual élites lived by the same ideas, analogies and commonplaces of thought, and the same old tales. Following a similar line of thought, Lucien Febvre's study, *Rabelais et le problème de l'incroyance au XVIe siècle*,[9] is devoted to defining the mental equipment ('outillage mental') of French thought at the time of Rabelais—the set of concepts that permeated life and art, thought and belief, long before and after Rabelais, and severely limited from the outset all intellectual adventure for even the freest minds. The work also of Alphonse Dupront [10] is one of the most recent pieces of research undertaken by the French school of history. Here, the idea of the crusade is considered—far beyond the fourteenth century, far beyond the 'actual' crusade—in its continuity as a lasting attitude, constantly renewed, passing through widely different worlds, societies and psychologies, touching even the nineteenth century with a final gleam. In what can still be called a neighbouring field, Pierre Francastel's book, *Peinture et société*,[11] taking the beginnings of the Florentine Renaissance as its starting point, points to the permanence of a geometrical treatment of pictorial space that nothing changed until the advent of cubism and conceptual painting at the beginning of our own century. The history of science, too, involves the construction of universes that constitute so many inadequate explanations, though each is regularly granted centuries of life. They are cast aside only after long service. The Aristotelian universe remained practically uncontested until Galileo, Descartes and Newton; then it faded in the face of a profoundly geometrized universe, which in turn crumbled, much later, in the face of the Einsteinian revolution.[12]

The difficult problem, which is only an apparently paradoxical one, is to show the long-term to be manifest in that field in which historical research has won undisputed success: economic systems—'economic cultures',[13] as some have said, referring to those age-old habits of thought and action, those tough, resilient frameworks of life that often defy all logic.

But let us argue from an example that can be rapidly analysed. Here on our doorstep, in Europe, is an economic system which can be expressed in terms of a few, fairly precise outlines and general rules: it maintained more or less the same position from the fourteenth to the eighteenth century until about 1750, let us say, for greater safety. For centuries, economic activity depended on demographically unstable populations, as is shown by the great ebb tide lasting from 1350 to 1450 and certainly by the one that lasted from 1630 to 1730.[14] For centuries transport was dominated by water and the ship; and any great landbarrier was a source of inferiority. In Europe, commercial growth took place along the coastal fringe, save for the exceptions proving the rule (the fairs of Champagne already in decline at the start of the period, or the fairs of Leipzig in the eighteenth century). This system had yet other characteristics: the primacy of the merchants; the leading role of precious metals, gold, silver and even copper (the constant damage done by them mitigated only at the end of the seventeenth century, if then, by the decisive development of credit); repeated destruction of large portions of the economy by seasonal agricultural crises; the fragility, in a word, of the very basis of economic life; finally, the apparently disproportionate role of one or two important elements of external trade: the Levantine trade from the twelfth to the fourteenth century and colonial trade in the eighteenth.

In these terms I have outlined or rather sketched, as others before me have done, the major features of mercantile capitalism in Western Europe as a long-term movement. In spite of all the evident changes that cut across them, these four or five centuries of economic life had a certain coherence that lasted until the upheavals of the eighteenth century and the industrial revolution, from which we have not yet emerged. Some features are common to these four or five centuries and remain constant, while around them, affecting other continuities, numerous crises and disturbances were changing the face of the world.

Among the different sorts of time that make up history, the long-term thus presents itself as a troublesome, complicated, often entirely new character. It will not be an easy matter to admit it into the very centre of our work and this will not only need the usual widening of the field of study and enquiry. Nor will our profession be able simply to make a decision and reap the appropriate benefits. For the historian, acceptance of the long-term means submission to a change of style and attitude; it implies an upheaval of thought and a new conception of the whole of social life; it means becoming familiar with time that is slow-moving, sometimes practically static. Only at this level, and at no other (I shall return to this point below), may one detach oneself from the exacting requirements of historical time to return later with fresh insight, filled with new interests, concerned with new questions. In a word, it is in relation to such vast expanses of slow-moving history and to this infra-structure that the totality of history is to be rethought. Every one of the thousand levels, the thousand explosions of historical time, can be grasped if one starts with this concept of depth and semi-immobility; that is the centre around which everything revolves.

I do not claim to have defined the historian's task in the preceding pages, but rather one conception of his task. It would be naïvely optimistic to think we have found real principles, definite frontiers and the right way at last, after the uncertainties of recent years. In fact every part of social science is constantly being transformed as a result of its own inner activity and the vigorous movement of the whole. History is no exception. So any form of complacency must be avoided; this is no time for disciples. It is a far cry from Charles Victor Langlois and Charles Seignobos to Marc Bloch, but since the time of Marc Bloch the wheel has never stopped turning. For me, history is the sum of all possible histories, a collection of occupational skills and points of view—those of yesterday, today and tomorrow.

The only mistake, in my view, would be to choose one of these histories to the exclusion of the others. This would be the old mistake of 'historizing'. As is well known, it will not be easy to convince all historians, and persuading the social sciences, so desperately eager to lead us back to the history of yesterday, will be even harder. We shall need time and a great deal of hard work to get all these changes and innovations accepted under the old heading of history. And yet a new 'science' of history has been born which will go on questioning and transforming itself. Its advent in France was marked by the appearance of the *Revue de synthèse historique* as early as 1900, then by the *Annales* from 1929 onwards. Historians were beginning to be attentive to *all* the human sciences. That is why our profession has unfamiliar frontiers and subjects of enquiry. What is more, we should not imagine that the barriers and differences still exist which only yesterday separated historians from social scientists.

Every social science, including history, is affected by all the others. They speak, or can speak, the same language.

In the year 1558, or in the year of grace 1958, getting a grasp of what the world is about means defining a hierarchy of forces, currents and individual movements, and refashioning the pattern of their totality. At each moment in the search, distinctions will have to be made between long-term movements and sudden growths, the latter being related to their immediate sources, the former to a long-term span. The world of 1558, so grim for France, was not born at the outset of that dismal year. Nor can this be said of 1958—which for us was another problem year. Each 'current event' brings together movements of different origin and rhythm: today's time dates from yesterday, the day before, and long ago.

3 *The dispute over the short-term*

True, these are platitudes. Yet the social sciences do not seem much inclined to undertake the search for lost time. Not that they can be formally convicted for always failing to accept history or time as necessary dimensions of their studies. Indeed, superficially they welcome us; the 'diachronic' analysis involving history is never absent from their theories.

But we must agree that, having made such devious acknowledgments, the social sciences, from inclination, instinctively, or even as a result of training, always tend to put aside the historical explanation;

they elude it by two practically contrary procedures: the one stresses the 'event' or 'actuality' to excess, being an empirical type of sociology scornful of all history, limited to the data provided by immediate enquiry; the other simply goes right beyond time, devising, under the heading of 'science of communication', a mathematical formulation of what are in fact non-temporal structures. This latter procedure, which is the most recent, is clearly the only one that can greatly interest us. But the event still has enough supporters for the two aspects of the question to be worth examining in turn.

We have expressed our mistrust of a history concerned solely with the event. But we must be fair: if there is such a thing as the sin of 'eventism', history is certainly not the only guilty defendant. All the social sciences commit the same error. Economists, demographers and geographers are split in their allegiance to yesterday and today, and the split is a mistake. The right thing would be to preserve an equal balance; for the demographer, this is an easy matter and indeed, for him, unavoidable; it is almost taken for granted by geographers (particularly our French geographers brought up in the Vidal tradition), but it is only rarely to be found among economists, imprisoned in the briefest actuality, between two time limits, one that goes back scarcely beyond 1945, and the other, the present day, extended into the immediate future only by plans and forecasts covering a few months or, at the most, a few years. I maintain that all economic thought is hampered by this restriction in time. Economists say that it is for historians to go back beyond 1945 in search of past economic systems; but they are depriving themselves of an excellent field of observation; they simply abandon it of their own accord, without denying its value. The economist is too much in the habit of rushing to serve the immediate present—and to serve governments.

The position of physical and social anthropologists is not as clear, nor as precarious. It is true that some have emphasized the impossibility (though every intellectual is committed to the impossible), and the pointlessness of introducing history into their subject. We can hardly say that this authoritarian rejection of history has been of great service to Malinowski and his disciples. In fact it is impossible to conceive of anthropology giving up all interest in history. Anthropology and history constitute the self-same adventure of the mind, as Claude Lévi-Strauss[15] likes to say. There is no society so time-worn that it does not, under scrutiny, reveal 'the claws of the event'; nor is there any society whose history has been entirely lost. Indeed, it would be unjust to exaggerate this complaint.

Our contention, however, regarding the short-term will be put forward fairly sharply when we come to research into contemporary life, moving in countless directions through the fields of sociology, psychology and economics. Both in France and abroad it is branching out everywhere. It rests, we might say, on continuous wagers on the indispensable value of present time, with its 'volcanic' heat and all its great resources. What could be the use of returning to historical time, deprived of its complexity, devastated by long silence and now merely reconstructed? Let us take note of that word 'reconstructed'. Is historical time really as 'reconstructed' as people make out? It is no doubt altogether too easy for the historian to pick out the essence of a past era; in the words of Henri Pirenne, he distinguishes 'important events' without difficulty, 'important events' no doubt meaning 'events that have had consequences'. This is an obvious simplification, and a dangerous one. But what would the traveller through the contemporary world not give to gain a perspective (or an advance of time) enabling him to lay bare and simplify the structure of present-day life, which a plethora of trivialities conceals from onlookers standing too close? Claude Lévi-Strauss maintains that an hour's conversation with one of Plato's contemporaries would teach him more about the coherence or incoherence of ancient Greek civilization than all our lectures on the classics.[16] I agree entirely. But the important point is that for years on end he has been listening to the voices of hundreds of Greeks rescued from silence. The historian has prepared the way. An hour in present-day Greece would teach him nothing, or next to nothing, about the coherences or incoherences of the present.

What is more, the researcher into the world of today arrives at the finer components of structures only if he too 'reconstructs', i.e. puts forward hypotheses and explanations, rejects reality in the crude form presented to him, cuts it up and goes beyond it—processes all entailing reconstruction, which lets us escape from the given pattern and re-arrange it. I doubt whether the sociological record of the present is any 'truer' than the historical picture of the past; and the further it tries to place itself from the 'reconstruction', the less 'true' it is.

Philippe Ariès[17] has insisted on the importance of distance and surprise in historical explanation: in the sixteenth century one comes up against a certain form of strangeness; strangeness especially for an observer four centuries away. How can we account for this discrepancy?

That is the whole problem. What I want to say is that surprise and distance—those important aids to comprehension—are both equally necessary for an understanding of that which surrounds you—surrounds you so evidently that you can no longer see it clearly. Live in London for a year and you will not get to know much about England. But, through comparison, in the light of your surprise, you will suddenly come to understand some of the most profound and individual characteristics of France, which you did not previously understand because you knew them too well. The past likewise provides distance from the present.

Historians and social scientists could, then, go on ringing the changes for ever, arguing about dead documents and evidence that is altogether too alive, the remote past and the too near present. I do not think this is a fundamental problem. Past and present illuminate each other. If one observes nothing but the limited present one's attention will be drawn towards anything that moves quickly, shines brightly, shows a new face, is noisy, or reveals its nature easily. A whole world of events as tedious as the one we meet in the historical sciences is there to ensnare the hasty observer—whether he is an anthropologist spending three months with a Polynesian tribe, or an industrial sociologist handing in copies of his latest enquiry or imagining that he will fully grasp some social mechanism by means of skilful questionnaires and combinations of punched cards. Social truth is a cunning prey that is not so easily outwitted.

Indeed, what interest is there, for students of the social sciences, in the journeys of a girl between her home in the sixteenth *arrondissement*, the home of her music teacher and the School of Political Sciences—as described in a vast and well conducted enquiry into the Paris region?[18] A pretty map is drawn. But the girl had only to study agriculture or go in for water-skiing and everything about these triangular journeys would change. It gives me pleasure to see the housing distribution of the employees of some great company illustrated on a map. But if I have no map showing their previous distribution, if the interval between surveys is insufficient to allow us to place everything in the context of a true movement, where is the problem without which an enquiry is a waste of time? The main interest of such enquiries, as far as the enquiry itself is concerned, lies, at the very most, in the accumulation of facts; and even they will not all be *ipso facto* valid for future work. Let us beware of art for art's sake.

I also doubt very much whether the study of any town can truly form the subject of a sociological enquiry (as was done for Auxerre[19] or Vienne in the Dauphiné[20]) unless the dimension of historical time is added. Any town, taken as a close-knit community that meets crises, truncations and breakdowns, with appropriate calculations, has to be considered within the complex of its surrounding region and the archipelago of its neighbouring towns (the historian Richard Hapke was one of the first to discuss the latter); thus it must be placed within the movement that gave life to the whole complex, perhaps far back in time. When registering exchanges between countryside and town or recording a situation of industrial or mercantile rivalry, can we think it trivial to find out whether we are dealing with a movement of recent origin, with a movement in full flight, or with one that is putting on a final spurt? Is it unimportant to know whether we are dealing with a movement resurging after a long delay or one that repeats itself endlessly? Is not such knowledge rather of the essence?

Let us conclude briefly: during the last ten years of his life Lucien Febvre is said to have often repeated these words: 'History is the study of the past and of the present.' Is not history, as the dialectics of duration, in its own way an explanation of the total reality of social life? And, therefore, an explanation of the present? In this respect, the lesson it teaches us is a warning—to be on our guard against the event, not to think merely within the short-term, not to think that those actors who make the most noise are the most authentic; there are other, silent ones. But who does not already know that?

4 *Communication and social mathematics*

Perhaps it was wrong to dwell on the troubled frontiers of the short-term period. Indeed, the debate that goes on there is of little interest and fails even to provide the surprise that might serve as a useful stimulus. The essential debate lies elsewhere; it is with those of our neighbours who have been won over to the very latest experiments of the social sciences, with 'communication' and mathematics as the main centres of interest.

But here the case will not be easy to plead; I mean that it will not be easy to place these endeavours in relation to historical time, with which, on the surface, they have no connection at all. In fact, no social study can fail to be connected with historical time.

In this discussion, at all events, any reader wishing to follow our train of thought (whether to agree or disagree) will do well to weigh for himself each term of a vocabulary which, though not entirely new, has been revived and rejuvenated in discussions that are still going on. Clearly there is nothing worth repeating about the event or the long-term. Not much to say about 'structures' either, although the word—like the thing—is not free from uncertainty and controversy.[21] It is pointless, too, to spend much time on the words 'synchronic' and 'diachronic'; they need no definition, although their role, in a specific social study, is more difficult to define than it appears. In fact, as I see it, there can hardly be such a thing, in historical terms, as perfect 'synchrony'; a momentary stop, suspending all durations, is almost absurd or (which comes to the same thing) totally artificial; in the same way a descent down the slope of time is conceivable only as a multiplicity of descents down countless rivers of time.

These brief reminders and warnings will suffice for the present. But we must be more explicit concerning 'unconscious history', 'models' and 'social mathematics', which are linked, or I hope soon will be linked, to a common approach on the part of all the social sciences.

'Unconscious history' is of course the history of the unconscious forms of all social life. 'Men make history, but are not aware of doing so.'[22] Marx's statement illuminates the problem, but does not explain it. In fact the whole problem of the short-term, 'micro-time' and the event, is with us once more, now under a new name. Men have always had the impression that the passage of time as lived by them is gained as things happen from day to day. Is not such conscious, clear history inadequate, as many historians have now long thought? Only yesterday linguists believed that everything could be learned from words. History had the illusion that it could learn everything from events. Any number of our contemporaries would be prepared to believe that every-thing has followed from the Yalta or Potsdam agreements, the chance events of Dien Bien Phu or Sakhiet-Sidi-Youssef or another event, important in another way, the launching of sputniks. Unconscious history proceeds along ways that lie far beyond these flashes of light. Let us admit, then, that there is such a thing as social unconsciousness lying some way away from us. Let us admit, too, until we have something better to go on, that such unconsciousness may, scientifically speaking, be considered richer than the flashing surface that our eyes are used to seeing; scientifically richer—that is to say, simpler, easier to exploit, if not to reveal. But distinguishing between the clear surface and the dark depths, between noise and silence, is difficult and chancy.

Let us add that 'unconscious history', as a field related to conjunctural time and, above all, to structural time, is often more clearly perceived than people will admit. Each one of us has the feeling that there is, beyond one's own life, a mass history, whose strength and impulses are perhaps more easily recognized than its laws or direction. And this awareness is not just a recent thing (for instance in economic history), even if it is today becoming livelier than before. The revolution, for in spirit it is a revolution, has consisted in coming face to face with this semi-darkness, and in making more and more room for it alongside the event, even at the expense of the event.

In this work of explanation, in which history is not alone (on the contrary, it has in this field merely followed and adapted to its needs the various points of view of the new social sciences), new instruments of learning and investigation have been constructed—'models', for instance, some better developed than others, some quite rough and ready. Models are nothing more than hypotheses, explanatory systems firmly constructed in the form of an equation or function: this equals that, or this determines that; this phenomenon never appears without this other one, and constant and close ties are shown between the two. The model that is then carefully set up will permit us to move through time and space and question other social environments of the same kind. Such is the recurrent value of the model.

These explanatory systems vary infinitely according to the temperament, calculations or aim of the user: they can be simple or complex, qualitative or quantitative, static or dynamic, mechanical or statistical. I have taken this last distinction from Claude Lévi-Strauss. Mechanical: the model is of the self-same dimensions as the directly observed reality, which is small, involving only small groups of men (this is the case when ethnologists deal with primitive societies). The calculation of averages is necessary for large societies where huge numbers come into play; these averages produce statistical models. But definitions of this sort, which are open to question, are not really important.

In my opinion, the essential thing is to define the role and limits of the model (which certain ventures run the risk of over-extending), before setting up a joint programme for the social sciences. Hence the need to confront models, too, with the idea of duration; for their depth of meaning and explanatory value depend, in my view, largely on the duration they imply.

It would be tempting to discuss the models of economists, but let us take some examples from models constructed by historians—rather clumsy, rudimentary ones, rarely made to the degree of precision required for a truly scientific law and never concerned with opening up a revolutionary mathematical language, yet still models of a sort.

We spoke above about mercantile capitalism between the fourteenth and eighteenth centuries: there we were dealing with one of many models taken from the work of Marx. It can be fully applied only to a given family of societies, for a given time, although it allows all manner of extrapolations.

It is different again for the model I sketched in a book written some time ago[23]—that of a cycle of economic development in Italian towns between the sixteenth and eighteenth centuries; they were first commercial, then 'industrial'; then they specialized in banking, this latter activity, the slowest to develop, being also the slowest to disappear. As the model in this sketch is in fact more limited than that provided by the structure of commercial capitalism, it is much easier to extend in time and space. It records a phenomenon (some would say a dynamic structure, but of course all historical structures are dynamic, at least in an elementary way), which is apt to reproduce itself in easily identified circumstances. Perhaps the same may be true of the following model, sketched by Frank Spooner and myself,[24] for the history of precious metals before, during and after the sixteenth century: gold, silver and copper (and credit, that extremely agile substitute for metal) are actors; the 'strategy' of one affects the 'strategy' of the others. It will not be difficult to use this model for situations outside the privileged and particularly vigorous society of the sixteenth century which we chose for our study. Have not economists tried, in dealing with the special case of today's under-developed countries, to confirm the old quantitative theory of money, which is also, in its way, a model?[25]

But the possible duration of all these models is still short in comparison to that of the model conceived by a young American social historian, Sigmund Diamond.[26] He was struck by the two languages used by the dominant class of big American financiers (the contemporaries of Pierpont Morgan); this class had an internal language for use within the class, and an external language (the latter being in fact a plea to public opinion, to which the financier's success is presented as the typical triumph of the 'self-made man', the necessary condition of the nation's own fortune). He sees in this use of two languages the habitual reaction of any dominant class that feels its prestige to be in danger and its privileges threatened; in order to mask its real self, it needs to have its fate identified with that of the City or the Nation, its particular interests with those of the public. In the same way Diamond explains the evolution of the idea of an English dynasty or a Roman Empire . . . The model thus conceived is obviously capable of spanning many centuries. It presupposes certain social conditions which are precise, but which recur very frequently in history: it is valid, therefore, for a much longer duration than the models mentioned previously, but at the same time it involves realities that are much narrower and more precise.

At its limit, as mathematicians would say, this sort of model comes near to the favourite, almost non-temporal models of mathematical sociologists—almost non-temporal, in the sense of travelling along the dark and unknown roads of the extremely long-term.

The preceding points are but an inadequate introduction to the science and theory of models. In this matter historians are a long way from taking up pioneering positions. Their models are hardly anything more than a bundle of explanations. Our colleagues are far more ambitious and advanced in their research, attempting to bring together the languages of information, theory, communication and qualitative mathematics. Their advantage, which is great, consists in opening the field to the subtle language of mathematics; the latter, however, is liable to slip out of control at the slightest inattention, and career off anywhere. Information theory, communication and qualitative mathematics can all be quite well grouped together and made to serve that much vaster subject, social mathematics. We shall just have to light our lantern as best we can.

Social mathematics[27] consists of at least three languages; these can be confused, and there is always the possibility that others may be introduced. There is no end to the imagination of mathematicians. At any rate, there is no single system of mathematics, nor is there any one subject of mathematics (except where some pretentious attitude is being adopted). 'We must not speak of algebra or geometry, but of a system of algebra or a system of geometry', as Th. Guilbaud says, and this does not simplify our problems or theirs. There are three languages then: the first is that of necessary facts (one fact is given and the other follows)— this is the domain of traditional mathematics; the second is the language of accidental facts, in use since the time of Pascal—this is the domain of probability calculation; finally, we have the language of conditioned facts—neither determined nor accidental, but subject to certain constraints and certain rules, as games are, and following the same paths as the concept of 'strategy' in the games of Von Neumann and Morgen-stern,[28] that triumphant concept of strategy, which for all its success is not content to rest on the principles and bold explorations of its founders. By making use of whole entities and groups, as well as by the actual calculation of probabilities, the strategy of games opens the way to 'qualitative' mathematics. At this point, the transition from observation to mathematical formulation is no longer forced to follow the difficult path of measurement and long statistical calculation. One can pass directly from social analysis to mathematical formulation and, I suggest, to the computer.

Obviously, material intended for such a machine has to be well prepared, for it cannot take in or digest every sort of food. Moreover a science of information has developed hand in hand only with actual machines and the laws governing their functioning in relation to communications' (in the most material sense of the word). The author of this article is by no means a specialist in this difficult field. Research conducted into the building of a translation machine, which he has followed from afar, but none the less followed, merely throws him together with others into a reverie. However, two facts remain: first, that such machines and such mathematical possibilities exist; second, that it is necessary to prepare social studies for social mathematics, which are no longer simply the old familiar mathematics: curves of prices, wages, births . . .

Now, if the exact form of the new mathematical mechanism often eludes us, the preparation of social facts for its use and the moulding of its patterns cannot escape our interest and attention. The preliminary treatment has till now almost invariably been the same: one chooses a restricted unit of observation, such as a 'primitive' tribe, or an isolated demographical case in which almost everything can be examined and explored at first hand; then one establishes all possible relationships and interplay between the elements observed. These rigorously-determined relationships produce the precise equations which mathematics later uses to discover all possible conclusions and extensions, resulting in a 'model' that summarizes them or, rather, takes them all into account.

Clearly, a thousand and one possibilities for research are opened up in these fields. But an example will be of more use than a long discourse. Claude Lévi-Strauss is an excellent guide—let us go with him. He will introduce us to a sector of his research, which we may call the science of 'communication'.[29]

'In any society,' writes Lévi-Strauss,[30] 'communication operates on at least three levels: females, goods and services, and messages.' Let us grant that these are different *languages*, at different levels, but languages just the same. Consequently, are we not entitled to treat them as languages, or even as *the* language and to associate them directly or indirectly with the sensational progress of linguistics, or rather, of phonology, which 'cannot fail to play a revolutionary role in respect to the social sciences, similar, for example, to that which nuclear physics has played in respect to the precise sciences'?[31] That is saying much, but it is sometimes necessary to say much. Just as history was caught in the trap of the event, linguistics was caught in the trap of the word, devoting itself to the relationship between words and the object, and to the historical evolution of words. It escaped via the phonological revolution. Staying this side of words, remaining in the material world, linguistics turned its attention to the phoneme, that is, the diagram of sound, and was thereafter indifferent to the meaning of the word, but careful to note its context, the sounds accompanying it, the groupings of these sounds, infra-phonemic structures, every underlying unconscious reality of language. The new field of work for mathematics was built up on a few dozen phonemes found recurring in all the languages of the world. And so linguistics, or at least a part of linguistics, in the course of the last twenty years, has left the world of social sciences and crossed the border to join the 'precise sciences'.

The search for the way to the difficult but salutary crossing of this border can be observed in the broadening of the meaning of 'language' to cover the elementary structures of kinship, myths, ceremonial and economic exchange; this is the achievement of Claude Lévi-Strauss, first in respect to matrimonial exchange, that primal language, so basic in human communication that there are no societies, primitive or otherwise, in which incest (that is, marriage within the narrow family unit) is not forbidden. There is, therefore, one common language. Beneath this language he has looked for a basic element, corresponding, one might say, to the phoneme, that element or 'atom' of kinship which our guide took into account in its simplest form in his thesis in 1949:[32] we must take it to mean man, wife, child, plus the child's maternal uncle. Starting with this quadrangular element and all known marriage systems of primitive societies—and these are numerous—mathematicians have to look for all possible combinations and solutions. With the aid of André Weill, the mathematician, Lévi-Strauss has managed to translate the anthropologist's observation into mathematical terms. The

31

model that appears must prove the validity and stability of the system and point to the solutions that the latter implies.

The procedure followed by this sort of research is plain—one must go beneath the surface of the thing observed to reach the zone of unconscious or barely conscious elements, then reduce this reality to its tiniest elements, perceiving the delicate, identical keys whose relationships with one another can be precisely analysed. It is at this 'microsociological' level (this *kind* of microsociological level—the qualification is mine) that one hopes to perceive structural laws of the most general kind, just as the linguist discovers his laws at the infraphonemic level and the physicist discovers his at the inframolecular level, that is, at the level of the atom.[33] This game can obviously be played in many other ways. Thus, what could be more instructive than to see Lévi-Strauss grappling with myths, this time, and, light-heartedly, with cooking (yet another language): he reduces myths to a series of elementary cells —'mythemes'; he reduces the language of cookery books (without taking himself very seriously) to 'gustemes'. Each time he is in search of deep, subconscious levels: while speaking, I am not concerned with the phonemes of my speech; when eating, I am not concerned with the 'gustemes' either, in a culinary sense, if there are such things as gustemes. And yet each time, the interplay of subtle and precise relationships is going on in my presence. Would the ultimate contribution of sociological research be to grasp these simple and mysterious relationships that lie beneath every language and translate them into a Morse code, I mean the universal language of mathematics? That is the ambition of new social mathematics. But, may I say, without smiling, that that is another *histoire*?

Let us bring duration back into the discussion. I have said that models are of varying duration: they have the same time-value as the reality they record. And for the social observer, this time aspect is of prime importance—for even more important than the profound structures of life are their breaking-points and their sharp or gradual deterioration under opposing pressures.

I have sometimes compared models to ships. For me, once the ship has been made, the whole interest lies in launching it, seeing whether it floats and then sending it out on the waters of time. Shipwreck is always the most significant moment. Thus the explanation for the interplay of precious metals that Frank Spooner and I put forward hardly seems to me to be valid before the fifteenth century. After the fifteenth century, the disturbances produced by precious metals were violent to a degree that had never before been known. So it is our task to look for the causes. Similarly we must examine why, when it moves downstream, the navigation of our ship, previously so easy, becomes difficult, then impossible, as it reaches the exceptional growth of credit in the eighteenth century. In my view, research must constantly move between social reality and the model, in a succession of readjustments and journeys ever patiently reviewed. Thus the model is both an attempt to explain a given structure, and an instrument with which one can examine it, and compare it, and test its solidity and its very life. If I constructed a model, starting from contemporary reality, I should want to locate it at once in reality, then make it move back in time, right to its birth, if possible. After that I should calculate its probable life-span as far as its next breaking-point according to the concomitant movement of other social realities. In other ways, using it as an element of comparison, I can move it through time and space in search of other realities capable of being illuminated by it.

Am I wrong in thinking that models produced by qualitative mathematics, in the form presented to us up till now,[34] would not easily lend themselves to such journeys, above all because they move on only one of the innumerable paths of time, that of the long, the *very long-term*, sheltered from accidents, conjunctures and breakdowns? Once more I shall return to Lévi-Strauss because his endeavours in this field seem to me to be the most intelligent, the clearest and, moreover, those best rooted in social experience, from which everything must branch out and to which everything must return. Each time, let it be noted, he considers a phenomenon that moves extremely slowly, as if outside time. All systems of kinship become permanently established because there is no human life possible beyond a certain rate of consanguinity, and because a small group of men, in order to live, must open itself up to the outside world: the prohibition of incest is a reality of long duration. Myths, being slow to develop, also correspond to extremely long-lasting structures. It is possible to collect the versions of the Oedipus legend without deliberately choosing the most ancient one, as the real problem is to line up the different variations and bring to light a profound connection between them. But suppose our colleague is interested in something else, perhaps not a myth, but the successive images and interpretations of 'machiavellianism', and is searching for the basic elements of a quite simple and very widespread doctrine, starting from its actual launching about the middle of the sixteenth century. At each moment, in this case, breakdowns and upheavals will take place in the very structure of machiavellianism, for this system lacks the theatrical, almost eternal solidity of the myth; it is sensitive to the tides of history and to its many storms. In a word, it is not merely travelling on the quiet and monotonous roads of the long-term . . . So the procedure recommended by Lévi-Strauss in the search for structures capable of being expressed mathematically is to be followed not only at the microsociological level, but also at the intersection of the infinitely small and the very long-term.

Apart from this, we may ask whether revolutionary qualitative mathematics is in fact condemned to follow only the paths of the very long-term. For if it is, then after a really hard struggle we should merely be coming back to truths that are too close to those of unchanging human nature: primitive truths, aphorisms of the wisdom of nations, some carping critics will say. Essential truths, we retort, which can illuminate the very foundations of all social life with a new light. But this is not the whole debate.

In fact I do not think that it is impossible to conduct these or similar endeavours outside the long-term. Not figures, but relationships, are being supplied by qualitative social mathematics; and these relationships must be quite rigorously defined before they can be given a mathematical sign, so that all the mathematical possibilities of these signs can be studied without any further reference to the social reality they represent. The entire value of the conclusions, then, depends on the value of the initial observation and the selection carried out in isolating essential elements from the reality observed, and determining their relationships at the heart of that reality. Thus we can well understand the preference of social mathematics for models which Claude Lévi-Strauss calls mechanical; that is to say, models which are set up following a study of small groups, where every individual can be directly observed and a very homogeneous social life allows one to define, unequivocally, human relationships that are simple, concrete and hardly variable.

So-called statistical models, on the other hand, are intended for vast, complex societies in which observation can be carried out only by using averages and traditional mathematics. But once these averages have been established, if the observer is also capable of establishing (on the group-scale and no longer on the scale of individuals) those basic relationships we spoke of which are necessary if the work of elaboration is to be performed by qualitative mathematics, there is no objection to using this method.

Up to the present, as far as I know, no such attempt has been made. But we are in the very early stages of experiment. For the time being, all experiments, whether in psychology, economics or anthropology, have been conducted in the way I have described with reference to Lévi-Strauss. But qualitative social mathematics will have proved itself only when it has taken on a modern society with all its tangled problems and various paces of life. Let us count on one of our mathematical sociologists being tempted by the venture; let us say, too, that the venture will inevitably provoke a revision of the methods followed up till now by the new mathematics; for the latter cannot restrict itself to what I should call, this time, the excessively long-term: it must come back to the multiple action of life with all its movements, durations, ruptures and variations.

5 *The historian's time and the sociologist's time*

As my incursion into the territory of non-temporal social mathematics comes to an end, here I am, back with time and duration. And, as an impenitent historian, I am again amazed that sociologists have managed to elude these two. But the fact is that their time is not ours: it is much less imperious, less concrete too, and never at the heart of their problems and reflections.

In fact the historian can never get away from historical time: time adheres to his thought like earth to the gardener's spade. True, he does dream of freeing himself from it. Gaston Roupnel,[35] in the anguish of 1940, expressed this in a way that is truly distressing for any sincere historian. The same point was made long ago by Paul Lacombe, another first-class historian: 'Time is nothing in itself, objectively, it is merely an idea we have.'[36] . . . But are these true escapes? During the course of a rather gloomy captivity, I personally fought hard to escape the time-sequence of those difficult years (1940–5). Rejecting events and the time period in which they were taking place was like setting myself aside and taking shelter so as to observe them from a distance, judge them better and not believe in them too much. The process is as follows: pass from the short- to the not-so-short-term and finally to the very long-term (if it exists, the latter can only be the time period of the sages); then, having arrived at this terminus, stop, consider every-thing anew and reconstruct, seeing everything revolve around oneself: a historian might well be tempted to do this.

But these successive flights of the imagination do not cut the historian permanently off from historical time, this dominates all since it is irreversible and flows at the same rhythm as the revolutions of the earth. In fact time periods which we distinguish form one cohesive whole: it is not duration itself that is the product of our mind, but rather the fragmentation of duration. These fragments are reunited at the end of our work. The long-term, the 'conjuncture' and the event fit together easily, because they can all be measured on one scale. And, of course, participating mentally in any one of these sorts of time means participating in all of them. The philosopher, being attentive to the subjective, interior aspect of the concept of time, never feels the weight of historical time in this concrete and universal sense. An instance is the time of the conjuncture, as described by Ernest Labrousse at the start of his book.[37] It is presented as a traveller of unchanging identity, who goes about the world imposing the same constraints, whatever country he may come to, whatever its political system or social order.

For the historian everything begins and ends with time, mathematical time, and as French historians say, *démiurge* time, about which it would be easy to be cynical; it is a time that is almost external to men, 'exogenous', as economists would say, driving men on, constraining them and sweeping away their individual, variously coloured times; indeed, it is the imperious time of the world itself.

Of course, sociologists do not accept this notion; it is too simple for them. They are much nearer to the 'dialectics of the time period' as presented by Gaston Bachelard.[38] Social time is simply a particular dimension of the social reality I contemplate. It is an internal part of this reality in the same way as it may be internal in the life of an individual, and it is also one of the external signs that it displays, one of the properties that distinguish it as an entity. The sociologist has no trouble with this sort of compliant time, which he can halt, divert into different channels, and set back in motion. Historical time, I repeat, would lend itself less readily to the dazzling double game of synchrony and diachrony: it hardly lets us see life as a mechanism whose movement can be arrested at any moment to present a static view of the whole.

The disagreement here goes deeper than it seems to do: the sociologist's time cannot be ours; the essential nature of our work forbids it. Our time is a means of measurement, like the economist's. When a sociologist tells us that every structure is subject to a constant process of destruction and self-renewal, we gladly accept this explanation which, besides, is confirmed by historical observation. But on the lines of our usual requirements, what we wish to know is the precise duration of such movements, and whether they are positive or negative. Economic cycles, the ebb and flow of material life, can be measured. A crisis in social structure must likewise be observable in time, and in its passage through time; it must be possible to locate it exactly, in itself, and, even more important, in relation to the movements of concomitant structures. The historian's real interest is in the meeting-points of these movements, their interaction and their breaking-points: and these are all things which can be recorded only in relation to the uniform time of historians, which is the general measure of all such phenomena; they cannot be recorded in relation to multiform social time, which is merely the particular measure of each taken separately.

Rightly or wrongly, the historian reacts with hostile attitudes like these, even when entering Georges Gurvitch's welcoming, almost fraternal brand of sociology. Did a philosopher[39] not describe Gurvitch only the other day as one who 'forces sociology towards history'? Now the historian recognizes neither durations nor temporalities, even in Gurvitch's system. Georges Gurvitch's vast social edifice (shall we say model?) is composed of five essential structures:[40] social strata, face-to-face groups, social groups, whole societies—and time. This last structure consists of 'temporalities' and is the newest of all, as well as the last; it is a sort of extra.

Georges Gurvitch's 'temporalities' are multiple. He distinguishes a whole series of them: slow-moving time of long duration, illusory time or 'surprise' time, time with irregular pulse, cyclical time or time that dances on the spot, time that falls behind itself, time that alternates between falling behind and going ahead, time that goes ahead of itself, and explosive time.[41] How could the historian let himself be persuaded by this? With this range of colours it would be impossible to reconstitute the single white light that he must have. He quickly realizes, too, that such chameleon time merely gives an extra touch of colour to categories that have already been defined. In our colleague's city, time, the last arrival, lodges quite naturally in the homes of the others; it adapts itself to the dimensions of their lodgings and requirements, according to strata, face-to-face groups, social groups or whole societies. It is a way of rewriting the same equations without altering them. Each social reality thus secretes its own time. What can we historians gain from all this? The mammoth architecture of this ideal city remains motionless. History is absent from it. World-time, historical time, is there, but, like Aeolus's winds, imprisoned in a goatskin. Sociologists are not opponents of history but of historical time—the reality which still remains powerful, even when one tries to divide it up and diversify it. The historian never escapes from this constraint, but sociologists almost invariably escape; they flee either to the perpetually fixed moment, which is, as it were, suspended above time, or to recurrent phenomena that belong to no single age; so they proceed according to attitudes of mind that are at opposite poles, confining themselves either to the strictest concentration on the event or to the very long-term. Is such escape legitimate? That is the real dispute between historians and sociologists, and even between historians of differing opinions.

I wonder whether this article, being perhaps too outspoken and, as is the custom with historians, too fully supplied with examples, will meet with the approval of sociologists and our other neighbours. I doubt it. In any case it is hardly necessary to repeat one's leitmotive as a conclusion, when it has already been emphatically stated. History, by its very nature, is called upon to give its special, privileged attention to duration and *all* the movements subject to which the latter may break down; but in this whole area of activity the long-term seems to us to be the most useful line of observation and thought that all the social sciences might pursue in common. Is it asking too much of our neighbours to hope that at some stage in their reasoning they may bring their findings and research back to this path?

For historians, who will not all share my opinion, this would mean a move into reverse: instinctively they give their preference to short-term history. It has the sacrosanct curricula of the universities to support it. In some recent articles,[42] Jean-Paul Sartre reinforces this point of view when he protests against all that is too simple and dogmatic in Marxism, doing so in the name of biographical detail and the multifarious reality of events. There is still much to say, after Flaubert has been 'placed' as a 'bourgeois', or Tintoretto as a 'petit bourgeois'. I quite agree. But the study of a specific case—Flaubert, Valéry or the foreign policy of the Gironde—brings Jean-Paul Sartre back every time to the structural, profound context. This process of enquiry leads from the surface to the depths of history and parallels my own preoccupations. It would parallel them better still if the hour-glass were turned twice, from the event to the structures and models back to the event.

Marxism is a whole collection of models. Sartre protests against the rigidity, the schematic, inadequate nature of models, and he does so in the name of the particular and the individual. I shall protest, as he does, more or less, not against the model, but rather against the use to which people have thought themselves entitled to put it. The genius of Marx, the secret of his enduring power, lies in his having been the first to construct true social models, starting out from the long-term. These models have been fixed permanently in their simplicity; they have been given the force of law and they have been treated as ready-made, automatic explanations, applicable in all places to all societies. Instead, by submitting them again to the changes wrought by time, we should reveal their true structure, which is strong and well-knit and would always recur, with subtle variations, blurred or brightened by the proximity of other structures, themselves definable in terms of other rules and models. In this way has the creative power of the most powerful social analysis of the last century been shackled. It will be able to regain its strength and vitality only in the long-term ... Shall I add that present-day Marxism seems to me to be the very image of the danger facing any social science devoted to the model in its pure state and for its own sake?

What I should like to emphasize by way of conclusion is that the concept 'long-term' is only one means of creating a common language for the social sciences. There are others. I have pointed out, as best I could, the endeavours of modern social mathematics. They attract me, but traditional mathematics, whose triumph is patent in economics—perhaps the most advanced of the social sciences—has not really deserved to fall into disrepute. Immense calculations await us in this classic domain, and there are whole series of computers and calculating machines daily being brought nearer to perfection. I believe in the usefulness of long-term statistics and in the need for a reverse journey by means of such calculations and research towards a past that grows more distant from day to day. The entire eighteenth century in Europe is strewn with working-sites, but the seventeenth is too, and even more so the sixteenth. Through their universal language,[43] statistics of undreamed duration are opening up for us the past of China. Admittedly, statistics simplify in order to clarify. But any science proceeds thus from the complicated to the simple.

However, let us not forget one last language, one last group of models; that is to say, let us not overlook the necessary reference of any social reality to the space in which it exists. The aim is to use geography or ecology without spending too much time on formulae to justify a choice between them. Geography, unfortunately, too often thinks of itself as an independent world. It needs someone like Vidal de la Blache, who, for this purpose, instead of the concepts of time and space, will use space and social reality. From then on the pace of geographical research will be set by the common problems of the social sciences. As for ecology, though he does not always admit it, the word is for the sociologist a way to avoid saying 'geography'; for he thus avoids the problems set by space and circumvents in particular those problems which space presents to the attentive observer. Spatial models are those maps on which social reality is projected and partially explained; they can be real models for any movement in time (especially the long-term) and for every category of social life. But, surprisingly, the social sciences are unaware of them. I have often thought that one of the chief assets to France in the domain of the social sciences was the school of Vidal de la Blache; and we shall never be able to make good our betrayal of its spirit and teachings. All the social sciences, for their part, will have to make room for an increasingly 'geographical conception of humanity';[44] Vidal de la Blache was pleading for this as early as 1903.

In practice—for this article has a practical aim—I should wish the social sciences, for the time being, to stop arguing so much about their common frontiers and about what is or is not a social science, what is or is not a structure. . . . Let them rather endeavour to discover any possible guide-lines, for collective research, and the subjects, too, which might allow them to converge. I personally see such guide-lines as mathematization, reduction to space, the long-term. . . . But I am curious to know what other specialists would propose. This article aims at raising and not at solving problems in which each one of us runs obvious risks, in stepping outside his own speciality. These lines are intended to provoke discussion.

Notes

1 *L'Anthropologie structurale*, Paris, 1958, *passim* and esp. p. 329 (English translation: *Structural Anthropology*, New York, 1963, *passim* and esp. pp. 298, 299).

2 *Annales*.

3 Jean-Paul Sartre, 'Questions de méthode', *Les Temps modernes*, 1957, nos. 139, 140.

4 Louis Halphen, *Introduction à l'histoire*, Paris, 1946, p. 50.

5 Cf. his 'Théorie générale du progrès économique', *Cahiers de l'I.S.E.A.*, 1957.

6 *Esquisse du mouvement des prix et des revenus en France au XVIIIe siècle*,
   2 vols, Paris, 1933.

7 Fully developed by René Clemens, *Prolégomènes d'une théorie de la structure
   économique*, Paris, 1952; see also Johann Ackerman, 'Cycle et structure',
   Revue économique, no. 1, 1952.

8 Ernst Robert Curtius, *Europäische Literatur und lateinisches Mittelalter*, Berne,
   1948. English translation, New York (Bollingen Foundation), 1953.

9 Paris, 1942.

10 *Le Mythe des Croisades; Essai de sociologie religieuse*, 1959.

11 Pierre Francastel, *Peinture et société: Naissance et destruction d'un espace
   plastique, de la Renaissance au cubisme*, Lyon, 1951.

12 Further arguments: I should like to bring into the discussion the following
   powerful articles which all illustrate the same point: Otto Brunner on the
   social history of Europe, *Historische Zeitschrift*, vol. 177, no. 3; R. Bultmann,
   ibid., vol. 176, no. 1, on humanism; Georges Lefebvre, *Annales
   historiques de la révolution française*, 1949, no. 114; F. Hartung, *Historische
   Zeitschrift*, vol. 180, no. 1, on enlightened despotism.

13 René Courtin, *La civilisation économique du Brésil*, Paris, 1941.

14 In France. In Spain the demographic ebb is noticeable from the end of the
   sixteenth century onwards.

15 *L'Anthropologie structurale*, p. 31.

16 'Diogène couché', *Les Temps modernes*, no. 195, p. 17.

17 *Le Temps de l'histoire*, Paris, 1954, esp. p. 298 et seq.

18 P. Chombart de Lauwe, *Paris et l'agglomération parisienne*, Paris, 1952, vol. 1,
   p. 106.

19 Suzanne Frère and Charles Bettelheim, 'Une ville française moyenne,
   Auxerre en 1950', *Cahiers des sciences politiques*, no. 17, Paris, 1951.

20 Pierre Clément and Nelly Xydias, 'Vienne-sur-le-Rhône. Sociologie d'une
   cité française', *Cahiers des sciences politiques*, no. 71, Paris, 1955.

21 See the *Colloquy on Structures*, by the École Pratique des Hautes Études,
   6th section, typewritten summary, 1958.

22 Quoted by Claude Lévi-Strauss, *L'Anthropologie structurale*, pp. 30–1.

23 *La Méditerranée et le monde méditerranéen à l'époque de Philippe II*, Paris,
   1949, p. 264 et seq.

24 Fernand Braudel and Frank Spooner, 'Les métaux monétaires et l'économie
   du XVIe siècle', *Rapports au congrès international de Rome*, 1955, vol. IV,
   pp. 233–64.

25 Alexandre Chabert, *Structure économique et théorie monétaire*, publication of
   the Centre d'Études Économiques, Paris, 1956.

26 Sigmund Diamond, *The Reputation of the American Businessman*,
   Cambridge, Mass., 1955.

27 See especially Claude Lévi-Strauss, *Bulletin international des sciences sociales*,
   UNESCO, VI, no. 4, and more generally the whole bulletin entitled *Les
   Mathématiques et les sciences sociales*, which is of great interest.

28 *The Theory of Games and Economic Behavior*, Princeton, 1944. Cf. the brilliant review by Jean Fourastié, *Critique*, Oct. 1951, no. 51.

29 All the remarks that follow are taken from his *L'Anthropologie structurale*.

30 Ibid., p. 326 (English translation, p. 296).

31 Ibid., p. 39 (English translation, p. 33).

32 *Les Structures élémentaires de la parenté*, Paris, 1949. See *L'Anthropologie structurale*, pp. 47–62.

33 *L'Anthropologie structurale*, pp. 42–3.

34 I speak only of qualitative mathematics, developed according to the strategy of games. A different argument would have to be employed in respect of classical models and those elaborated by economists.

35 *Histoire et destin*, Paris, 1943, *passim*, esp. p. 169.

36 *Revue de synthèse historique*, 1900, p. 32.

37 Ernest Labrousse, *La Crise de l'économie française à la veille de la Révolution française*, Paris, 1944, Introduction.

38 *Dialectique de la durée*, 2nd ed., Paris, 1950.

39 Gilles Granger, 'Évènement et structure dans les sciences de l'homme', *Cahiers de l'Institut de Science Économique Appliquée*, Série M, no. 1, pp. 41–2.

40 See my article, doubtless over-polemical, 'Georges Gurvitch et la discontinuité du Social', *Annales*, 1953, 3, pp. 347–61.

41 Cf. Georges Gurvitch, *Déterminismes sociaux et liberté humaine*, Paris, 1955, pp. 38–40 and *passim*.

42 Jean-Paul Sartre, 'Fragment d'un livre à paraître sur le Tintoret', *Les Temps modernes*, Nov. 1957, and the article previously quoted.

43 Otto Berkelbach van der Sprenkel, 'Population statistics of Ming China', *Bulletin of the School of Oriental and African Studies*, 1953; Marianne Rieger, 'Zur Finanz und Agrargeschichte der Ming Dynastie 1368–1643', *Sinica*, 1932.

44 P. Vidal de la Blache, *Revue de synthèse historique*, 1903, p. 239.

Three

The so-called 'Price Revolution': Reflections on 'the Italian Situation'

Carlo M. Cipolla

'The Price Revolution'—such is the imposing label that has been given to the history of prices in the sixteenth century. It has certainly made its mark. There is no book on economic history that fails to adopt it and use it in order to explain, by means of its 'Open, Sesame' effect, the entire economic history of the beginning of the modern era.

The success of this formula is partly due to the extraordinary simplicity of conception which it represents. When one talks of 'the price revolution' one always implies two very simple things: between the beginning of the sixteenth century and the beginning of the seventeenth, a 'revolutionary' rise in prices took place; this rise was caused by the tremendous influx of American gold and silver. In his famous book on the economy of the Mediterranean in the age of Philip II, Fernand Braudel gives this concept his blessing, underlining 'the violence and length of this revolution', stating that 'there is no possible doubt about the effect of the influx of gold and silver from the New World . . . the coincidence of the curve of influx of precious metals from America and the curve of prices throughout the sixteenth century is so clear that there seems to be a physical, mechanical link between the two. Everything was governed by the increase in stocks of precious metals.'

This is the traditional view: a line runs from Jean Bodin to Hamilton (and if Hamilton shows an advance on Bodin from the statistical point of view, we must confess that he has not advanced an inch in monetary theory). There is no real doubt that this tradition conveys some truth. But how much?

First of all, let us examine the 'violence' of the rise and the 'revolution' in prices. Let us take the price index calculated for Florence by Parenti. It is an adequate index. A vast investigation that I am conducting in Lombardy together with my friend Aleati shows that Parenti's index is confirmed by Lombard material. So the Parenti index, standing at 100 for the 1610–20 period, is 50 in 1552 (the beginning of the 'revolution'), and 103 in 1600 (the culminating point of the 'revolution'). Consequently, within a period of about fifty years one finds an increase of 106 per cent, that is to say, scarcely more than a 2 per cent average increase per year (and if one were to calculate the composite average rate, one would obtain only 1·5 per cent). An examination of the documents shows that the increase behind the general rise of the index from 50 to 103 was not regular and continuous. On the contrary, it shows alternating periods of rise and fall as follows:

Period	Average annual movement (per cent)
1552–1560	+5·2
1560–1565	−1·2
1565–1573	+3·3
1573–1590	−0·4
1590–1600	+3·1
1600–1617	−0·8

For purposes of comparison let us now, from Rostow, take the movement of prices in England in the nineteenth century, the century of 'monetary stability':

Period	Average annual movement (per cent)
1791–1815	+1·8
1815–1847	−1·4
1847–1873	+0·6
1873–1900	−1·5
1900–1912	+1·5

Any comparison of these two indices can be only very crude: they have been calculated differently, for different products. However, in order to arrive at an approximate conclusion and to clarify our ideas, the parallel may be attempted—it is quite instructive.

It is certain that increases were sharper in the sixteenth century than in the nineteenth. But still the 'great revolution' seems rather diminished in size. The most marked rise occurs between 1552 and 1560; it reaches 5·2 per cent per year. There is no doubt that this rate is inflationary. But it lasted only eight years. The two other periods showing an increase give rates scarcely in excess of 3 per cent, and they do not last longer than eight and ten years. Periods of increase in the nineteenth century were less intense but lasted longer (twenty-four, twenty-six and twelve years).

Besides, there is another element in the sixteenth-century figures that deserves our attention: during the long periods of decrease, prices gave evidence of extraordinary resilience. Given a taste for paradox, one might say that the rise (avoiding the term 'revolution') in prices in the sixteenth century was due to the fact that they did not fall during periods of decrease. In the nineteenth century a long period of increase was always followed by a long period of decrease, each being more or less equally intense and equally long, so that at the end of the century prices were no higher than at the beginning. In the sixteenth century, however, prices rose rapidly during long periods of increase and fell at a reduced speed during long periods of decrease, so that at the end of the period they stood higher than at the beginning.

This is where the role of American gold and silver becomes apparent. It created a limit below which prices could not fall during the long periods of depression: and it acted as a stimulus to even greater activity during the long periods of development (just as it acted as a buffer against increases in interest rates during periods of development, and aggravated the fall in interest rates during periods of depression).[1] It had the effect of intensifying or restraining *general movements*. This was certainly an important effect, but it expressed and revealed itself only through other *movements*: above all, movements of investments. These act as the true springs of movements in prices. They cannot be overlooked or relegated to second place.

Italian economic history in this period is highly significant in this respect. The long period of marked increase lies between 1552 and 1560, showing an average annual rise (non-composite) of 5·2 per cent. That is well enough. But it is very hard to explain this rise, in its entirety anyway, in terms of the influx of American gold and silver. Italy did not receive exceptional quantities of precious metals during this period; rather, as far as we can tell, she received less then than during the following decades. But the country had to be rebuilt. The war that had reigned there throughout the first half of the century had utterly destroyed Italy. With the return of peace, the country recovered: this entailed material and demographic reconstruction. American metal was not yet abundant, but prices rose at a precipitate pace, for people spent what they had in order to rebuild. We thus reach a conclusion that rather weakens the old theory: the most important rise in the 'revolution' was due much more to the country's work of reconstruction than to American silver.

The situation changes after 1570. As Professor Braudel has demonstrated in masterly fashion, using a truly remarkable abundance of documents, the Mediterranean, and Italy in particular, was invaded by precious metals from America after 1570. The Spanish Crown, for reasons that we need not discuss here, diverted its treasures towards the Mediterranean: 'that enormous swelling of the traffic in coinage and credit throughout the western Mediterranean, which had been chosen as the imperial route for silver'. But it is precisely the year 1570 that marks the beginning of a period in which prices fall. The mass of money released on to the market succeeded in holding back the fall in prices to an average rate of 1·4 per cent per year. But none the less prices tended to fall. There are factors in economic movements that operate in a negative sense. Precious metals from America slowed down the fall in prices: but they did not stop it.

The problem is to find out what connection there is 'between the curve showing the influx of precious metals from America and the price curve for the whole sixteenth century'. One small fragment of Italian economic history seems to show that the 'connection' was not—at least as far as Italy was concerned—either as mechanical or as obvious as Braudel claims. Standing between the gold curve and the price curve were men, with their desires, preferences and needs.

Note

1 If there was a 'revolution', it was a 'revolution in the interest rate' rather than a 'revolution in prices'. In fact, at the end of the sixteenth century the interest rate was seen for the first time in history to stand below 5 per cent on some European markets. This 'innovation' was doubtless a result of the influx of gold and silver from America. See C. M. Cipolla, 'Note sulla storia del tasso di interesse', *Economia Internazionale*, vol. V, 1952.

Four

More about the Sixteenth-century Price Revolution

Alexandre R. E. Chabert

Adam Smith, author of *The Wealth of Nations* (1776), wrote concerning American gold and silver and the rise in prices in the sixteenth and seventeenth centuries: 'The discovery of the abundant mines of America seems to have been the sole cause of this diminution in the value of silver in proportion to that of corn. It is accounted for accordingly in the same manner by everybody; and there has never been any dispute either about the fact itself or about the cause of it.'[1] Fifty years earlier, Richard Cantillon, another economist, an Irishman of French origin, had expressed the same opinion: 'Everybody agrees that an abundance of money or an increase in the exchange of money, raises the price of everything. The quantity of money brought from America to Europe in the last two centuries bears out the truth of this statement.'[2] These two quotations do not constitute the foundation of the famous quantity theory of money—this was put forward as early as the sixteenth century by Jean Bodin at the time of his famous controversy with Malestroit in 1568—but they do mark its eventual triumph. Since that time there has been nothing much worth mentioning on the subject. Recently, studies by Earl J. Hamilton on Spain and by Fernand Braudel on the entire Mediterranean area in the sixteenth century have given the old theory statistical and historical confirmation, though there was no real need for this. But there are limits to all theories and they all have their opponents. Did the sixteenth century obey the quantitative laws, as has commonly been thought, or not?

That amiable economic historian, Carlo M. Cipolla, recently disputed the usual explanation.[3] And his lively article, with its provocative title, deserves attention; it forces us to reconsider a classic subject—and there is considerable merit in that. It is true, of course, that the quantity theory could never be applied to the complex nature of money and prices in the capitalist world of today and embrace it in its entirety and in every detail. Of course not . . . but the sixteenth century is not the present day. That is the very problem we should like to take up again and discuss step by step—and perfectly frankly—with our Italian colleague.

Carlo Cipolla, then, contests the quantity theory; he tries to show that the so-called price revolution in the sixteenth century, for Italy at least, is nothing more than a half-truth, or a myth. Our colleague uses two kinds of argument in support of his view with considerable finesse; they are statistical and economic. Let us first try to summarize them.

1 There is nothing exceptional in the price rise in sixteenth-century Italy, as revealed by recent statistical enquiries (the indices drawn up by Giuseppe Parenti for Florence and Siena, and the 'vast' enquiry being carried out by Carlo Cipolla and Giuseppe Aleati on Lombardy). It reached its peak in the second half of the sixteenth century, between 1552 and 1560. Now between these dates the annual rate of increase is barely 5·2 per cent. For the other two periods of increase the rate drops to 3 per cent. And here we have periods of increase lasting only eight or ten years. We may conclude with our colleague that the flow of American gold and silver into Italy was far from causing a true *revolution* in prices. We must not go beyond fact; we should dispense with the misleading term 'revolution'; it is handy, but over-dramatic. In short, the quantity theory—i.e. the quantity of bullion—did not operate in the case of Italy, or if it did, our author concedes, it acted simply as a brake to falling prices. 'Given a taste for paradox, one might say that the rise (avoiding the term "revolution") in prices in the sixteenth century was due to the fact that they did not fall during periods of decrease.'

2 Thus the first point made is that the rise was not enormous. Moreover, the rise, when it came, took place at the beginning of the period under discussion (1552–60), precisely at a time when the quantity of bullion imported into Italy was small. Yet after 1570, when the flow of bullion becomes considerable, as is shown in work carried out by Fernand Braudel, there is a drop in prices. Monetary phenomena thus belie the doctrines and forecasts of the quantity theory; for, as every-

body knows, according to its simple laws prices rise in proportion to the amount of gold and silver money made current. This of course is a blow to the adherents of the old explanation.

Carlo Cipolla concludes: the role of American gold and silver was to intensify or restrain general movements in the economy. . . . Nothing more than that; but that, of course, is plenty. . . .

Cipolla's remaining concern is to explain price fluctuation; since money is not the guilty party, investment is taken to task, the investment required for the reconstruction of Italy, which had been destroyed and gradually depopulated during the wars of the first half of the sixteenth century. In other words, the cause of the movement in prices is not to be found in the varying quantities of money brought into circulation, but in the multiple springs of economic activity, which are also of variable strength. This is the argument used by all the *opponents of the quantity theory* of every age and every country.[4] Is it any more convincing for all that? However brilliant it may be, such an interpretation does not accord with contemporary accounts,[5] nor with the results of modern economic analysis. This is what I shall now try to prove with the support of figures and by consideration of the actual data; after that I shall present my reasoned doubts regarding the *logical* validity of the arguments put forward.

Let us now take up the arguments against the quantity explanation. They are twofold; our reply will likewise be twofold. It will first move into the field of statistics, then the field of economics, and we offer our apologies in advance for making a distinction that is convenient but somewhat artificial. This distinction is not really of our own making. In default of any research conducted personally by myself there is of course no question of my arguing with Carlo Cipolla about the representative nature of the statistical indices for Italy. And I have no desire to do so. We must accept his figures as a reliable gauge. And in this matter I think that we can have complete confidence in our colleague and indeed in all Italian historians. The bone of contention does not lie here, as far as I am concerned. It is in the interpretation of these figures. Contrary to the statements made in the article we are criticizing, an annual rise of 5 per cent, or even 3 per cent, represents a not inconsiderable rate—and that is the essential point—especially when one recalls the previous behaviour of prices, the chief characteristic of which was very great stability; and the significance of this 5 per cent or 3 per cent rise is brought out even more strikingly if we consider this aspect of the sixteenth century, whose most striking feature is long stagnation. It was this ossified *ancien régime* in prices which, once it finally began to loosen up, opened the way for a long-lasting rise, giving historians the impression that something new, even a revolution, had occurred. This rise is in itself a considerable fact; and, an even more considerable fact, it had the same impact on contemporary observers. So the annual rate of increase was, in my opinion, quite appreciable; this explains why, in spite of cyclical falls between 1550 and 1560, the upward trend always predominates, fixed each time at a higher level than before (which the author himself acknowledges). However, if this 50 per cent increase affecting Italian prices between 1550 and 1600 seems slight in comparison with the price movements in other western countries—Spain and France—the explanation is not so difficult to see, and it certainly does not affect the validity of the quantity theory. Why go for that?

Precious metals spread across Europe as a result of expenditure on goods and services by the Spaniards, who possessed this 'manna'—it is unnecessary to dwell on the processes and channels by which the spread was effected.[6] Nations dealing directly with the Spaniards—the French, Dutch and English—benefited more than others from this exceptional situation. The Italians, especially in the north, were less advantageously placed for Iberian trade and did not derive such benefit from it. Stocks of gold in Italy grew from 1570 onwards as a result of political and strategic consignments of precious metals. The 'moderate' extent of the rise in prices in Italy in the second half of the sixteenth century might then be explained by the hoarding of precious metals for political ends. In any case, in the absence of any full statistical information on the influx of American gold and silver, the limited extent of the rise in prices in Italy does not prove much. We must first be in a position to compare the movements of the additional mass of money pouring on to the Italian markets with actual price movements, before we can come to any valid conclusions about them either way. Investigation of this aspect is still wide open. . . .

If the statistical interpretation of the figures seems inconclusive, what shall we say of the economic argument, which is undoubtedly far less convincing? In fact the assumption that the mainspring of price fluctuations in Italy, upwards and, I suppose, downwards, is to be found in investment—that is, in the process of economic creation— does not stand up to any moderately penetrating economic and historical analysis. While it is true that the quantity theory of money in its traditional form (or even in its modern form) asserts that there is a relationship between prices and precious metals, it maintains at the same time that growth in production prevents any influx of precious metals from having its full effect.[7] In fact numerous testimonies agree not only that there was a rise in prices in Europe in the sixteenth century, but that a general expansion of economic activity also took place.[8] These two aspects are complementary. As long as a 'national' economy is in a state of under-employment, precious metals pouring on to the market act as supplementary purchasing power and a factor in expansion. But as soon as the economy in question reaches its production limit, any introduction of new money leads to a rise in prices. In short, the weaker the production capacity, the sooner the threshold of inflation is reached and crossed. In this respect the under-developed countries of the present day offer us a convincing comparison with economic life in Europe in the sixteenth and seventeenth centuries. In the under-developed regions, characterized by rigidity of production, in the countries where people have less than their essential requirements,[9] any creation of monetary purchasing power sparks off a rise in prices as spending proceeds.[10]

In any economy with a limited and therefore rigid production capacity, an increase in prices can take place instantly or, one might say, mechanically. It is not at all necessary for there to be an influx of additional money reserves before such phenomena are sparked off. Sometimes an increase in the supply of precious metals is sufficient in itself. Conversely, in other situations a large influx of money may very well still fail to answer the needs of business expansion. In that case, the main tendency as far as prices are concerned will be an increase in the value of money, which will be more in demand, and so there will be a drop in prices, precisely because of the lack of metal.[11] But in either case, I repeat, the operation of the quantity theory of money is visible only where there is *constant* economic activity,[12] which is precisely the case for areas with fixed production output, such as Europe in the sixteenth century.

These considerations bring us back to Carlo Cipolla's interpretation; as we have said, he takes investment to be the mainspring of price variation after 1562. This argument seems to me untenable; what can such investment mean for an Italy that had been impoverished and depopulated by war? Such a concept is vague even in reference to the present day, and is even vaguer for the past. Did investment represent building reconstruction, as is probable? Or the reconstruction or founding of factories or workshops? What we know about the labour force leaves us sceptical about the *extent* of the ensuing production effort. The rigidity of production processes determined a rise in prices in Europe in those days, once the full employment level was reached: the same is true of under-developed countries today. This seems to us to be the explanation of the 'precipitate' rise in prices in 1550, referred to by our colleague when he writes: 'American metal was not yet abundant, but prices rose at a precipitate pace, for people *spent* what they had in order to rebuild' (my italics [Chabert]). In the circumstances the mainspring of the rise was not reconstruction (i.e. investment), but spending. The monetary holdings of various individuals who had been made rich by the new, though still modest, consignments from America poured into circulation in exchange for various products or services. The Italian economy, of which the very most one can say is that it was convalescent, was hardly able to respond to such a supply of additional money, and the rise continued as long as the Italian economy did not attain stability and remained unable to respond to a growing demand for goods.

However, as soon as the rhythm of expansion had reached a certain level and the influx of money had, for better or worse, answered the growing monetary needs of the Italian economy, there is nothing surprising about an ensuing drop in prices. . . . Thus it is after 1570, the year in which a growing influx of gold and silver coincides with a drop in prices. This explanation is all the more likely since the demographic 'reconstruction' begun in 1550, which our colleague mentions, can only have taken full effect twenty years later. Demographic growth, on taking full effect, demands an increase in the total amount of currency. Metals from America, even in larger quantities than before, were probably unable to answer the new demands of Italian economic life and demography. Thus might one explain the apparent paradoxes, emphasized by our colleague, which seem to weaken the quantity theory; there was, then, a moderate influx of gold and silver in 1550 and a wholesale increase in prices; after 1570 came a huge influx of bullion accompanied by a drop in prices.

Even if price movements in Italy are as their commentators describe them, they are far from invalidating the application of the quantitative theory *to that period*. Let us repeat—the quantitative theory postulates a certain economic structure. The simpler this structure is, or even the more rudimentary it is, the more rigid is productive capacity and the more clearly the classical monetary phenomena predicted by the quantitative theory stand out. This time-honoured model, this structural framework, need not be overthrown.

You will perhaps say that all this is nothing but an automatic, mechanical game. That indeed seems to have been the case in sixteenth-century Europe. Yet this game, however harsh and mechanical it may be, does take man and his reactions into account. François Simiand said so a long time ago: 'It is clear from all this that we have proceeded as follows: the antecedent that we have taken into consideration is the variation in precious metals, whether these are produced or imported; between this antecedent and its economic consequences as perceived by us, we have placed price movements together with the material increase in products and services. In all this let us acknowledge man as the intermediary, that is, the being, or rather the human beings, who have these precious metals at their disposal and use them in a certain way, so that from them certain economic movements result.'

Of course the discussion is not closed. In a debate which will never end I thought it might be useful to strike another note. Now it is up to the readers of *Annales* and historians to form an opinion.

Notes

1 *The Wealth of Nations*, ed. Cannan, London, 1904, vol. 1, p. 191.
2 *Essai sur la nature du commerce en général*, ed. H. Higgs, London, 1931, p. 160.
3 See above, p. 43.
4 For a history of the evolution of the quantitative theory of money, see E. James, *Histoire de la pensée économique au XXe siècle*, pp. 212–16.
5 Cf. Bodin, *Réponses . . .*, 1572 edition, re-edited by Yves le Branchu, vol. I, p. 94 in particular.
6 Cf. F. Simiand, *Recherches anciennes et modernes sur les mouvements généraux des prix du XVIe au XIXe siècle*, p. 493.
7 Montesquieu himself saw this when he wrote: 'If gold and silver have increased in Europe in a ratio of one to twenty since the discovery of the Indies, the price of food and merchandise should have risen too from one to twenty. But if the quantity of merchandise has risen in a ratio of one to two, then the price of this merchandise must have risen one to twenty and fallen one to two, so that, in consequence of this, the total price increase stands at one to ten' (*L'Esprit des lois*, Book 22, ch. 8).
8 Cf. Harsin, *Les Doctrines monétaires et financières en France aux XVIe et XVIIe siècles*.

9 J. de Castro, *Géopolitique de la faim*, Paris, 1952.

10 See our *Structure économique et théorie monétaire*, Paris, 1956. The argument sustained in this work has met with confirmation in the observations of certain well-informed people from these regions. Here is what Mr Vu-Quoc-Thuc, governor of the Bank of Viet Nam, wrote to us on 18 August 1956: 'I myself have had the opportunity of studying the economic behaviour of Viet Nam and I am pleased to tell you that my conclusions agree completely with yours. In Viet Nam, for instance, the central Bank has only to inject a little more money into currency for the market to feel it soon afterwards. Conversely, the deflationary policy I am at present pursuing, produces incontestable effects on prices. So all this confirms your argument and I entirely share your opinion when you compare the structure of under-developed countries with that of eighteenth-century Europe.'

11 We should recall that a rise in prices indicates a drop in the value of money, as the money available exceeds monetary demand. The phenomenon is reversed in the event of prices falling.

12 According to the classic formula of Fisher: $MV + M^1V^1 = PT$; V (velocity of circulation) and T (transactions) are assumed constant for the quantity theory to apply.

Five

Price and Wage Movements in Belgium in the Sixteenth Century

C. Verlinden, J. Craeybeckx, E. Scholliers

The history of prices and wages in the modern era in Belgium, or, if the name is preferred, the southern Low Countries, is still in its infancy. Practically all that Belgium has to set alongside the numerous excellent publications that have appeared in France, Germany, England, Holland and elsewhere, are the documents that were collected more than half a century ago by H. Van Houtte. They are concerned with the prices of certain agricultural products in a few markets in the county of Flanders between 1381 and 1794,[1] and there are no comments or charts. For the sixteenth century, to which the present article is devoted, M. I. Delatte's article on Hainault[2] should also be mentioned, along with references that occur in works of a more general nature by J. Lejeune and, in particular, J. Ruwet.[3] All this adds up to very little and it is not surprising that such a state of affairs appeared in the end quite unacceptable to certain Belgian historians, who quite recently asked for and obtained the support of their government in creating an Inter-university Centre for the history of prices and wages in Belgium in modern times.[4] The Centre's aim is to collect material in the style of Beveridge and Post-humus, etc. The time period to be covered stretches from the late Middle Ages to 1850. So its activity centres on the modern period but extends beyond it at both ends. So far only preparatory study has been done.

The work that has been under way for the last few years in the Modern History Seminar of Ghent University must also be seen as part of the preliminary stage in the investigation. The aim of this article is to present some of the initial results and make known some views on the sixteenth century which the authors have based on research carried out by three groups of students. One of these students, M. A. Wyffels, has written an unpublished first degree thesis from which we have taken a certain amount of material. In addition, the account of wages in Antwerp that rounds off this article is the work of M. E. Scholliers, who is preparing a doctor's thesis on prices and wages in Antwerp in the sixteenth century.

On making a graph of five-yearly average prices of wheat in Flanders between 1385 and 1794 from the data provided in H. Van Houtte's tables (Fig. 1),[5] one is struck by the extraordinary speed at which they rise in the sixteenth century. Before and after the sixteenth century, despite some pronounced ups and downs, the curve on the whole follows a fairly horizontal path, but the period from 1500 to 1600 is marked by a very steep climb, and the few brief occasions on which the curve levels out do not halt the general rise. The seventeenth century starts with a slight drop; then comes a recovery with prices exceeding the highest level attained in the previous hundred years; while the eighteenth century is marked by a gradual, though sometimes rather jerky, return to the level reached at the end of the sixteenth century. Although we are dealing here with unadjusted actual figures, we see at once, from the place occupied by the sixteenth century in the overall curve, that no other period between the late Middle Ages and the close of the modern era raises as many basic questions for the historian of prices—and wages—as the one that now forms the subject of our study.

One of the first questions to occur to any student used to this type of research is whether there may be a cyclical rhythm in price movements in the southern Low Countries in the sixteenth century.

Taking Van Houtte's figures once more as our basis, if we draw a graph of prices fetched by a measure (*heu*) of wheat in Flanders at the Ghent, Bruges, Courtrai, Alost and Rupelmonde markets, in Paris pounds, between 1499–1500 and 1599–1600, and if we extract from it the long-term curve according to the mobile averages method used by E. Labrousse for the eighteenth century (Fig. 2),[6] we shall have the necessary starting-point for a graph analysis of cyclical movements of wheat prices in Flanders (Fig. 3). But it is important to realize that E. Labrousse based his calculations on thirteen-year periods, comprising the six years prior to the individual year which he sets against the long-term average, that year itself, and the six years that follow.[7] The thirteen-year period represents, approximately, two complete cycles, that is to say it contains an equal proportion of years of rise and fall in the cyclical process. However, in the sixteenth century the rise quickens so much that the thirteen-year period, which is better suited to the steady tempo of the eighteenth century, soon proves to be inadequate. Curiously enough, the empirical choice of a nine-year period has given results that tally far better with the actual figures. Fig. 2, with the long-term movement founded on thirteen-year periods, brings out only a few peaks above the average, towards the close of the century.

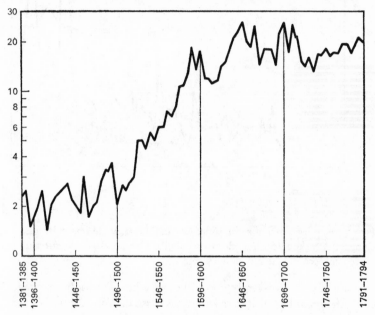

Figure 1 Five-year averages for wheat prices per measure (*heu*) in Flanders (Ghent, Bruges, Courtrai, Alost, Rupelmonde) in Paris pounds, 1381–1794. Logarithmic scale.

The highly characteristic movement shown in Fig. 3 is obtained by working on nine instead of thirteen years—these nine years consist of the year on which our attention is focused and two groups of four years before and after. This brings out the cyclical movement particularly clearly. The peaks came in the years 1502–3, 1513–14, 1521–2, 1531–2, 1545–6, 1556–7, 1565–6, 1573–4, 1586–7 and 1595–6; in each case these dual figures cover a period between two harvests. The average length of a cycle of rise and fall is 10·3 years. Almost invariably, between the ten-yearly peaks there are lesser peaks—for example 1507-8, 1516-17, and so on. . . .

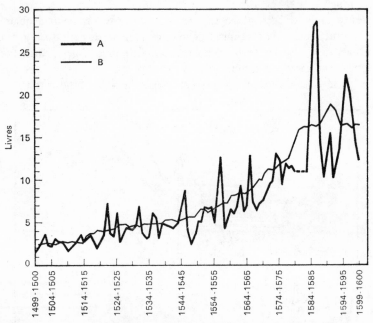

Figure 2 A, price of wheat per measure (*heu*) in Flanders at the Ghent, Bruges, Courtrai, Alost and Rupelmonde markets, in Paris pounds. B, the long-term movement according to mobile averages.

So there were five-yearly rises, denoting crises. The mobile averages curve shown in Fig. 2, as stated above, is based on Van Houtte's figures for Flanders, that is to say on market prices recorded on three separate occasions during the year after harvest. But until further information is produced we can take them as valid for the whole of the Low Countries; justification for so doing is provided, for instance, by a comparison with I. Delatte's data for Hainault and J. A. Sillem's data for Utrecht.[8] Years of crisis are the same for all three sets of data, though the total rise in prices throughout the century varies slightly from one to another.[9]

Among the cyclical crises that stand out so clearly in Fig. 3, one might be tempted to explain those of 1531–2 or 1565–6 as the result of navigation problems in the Sound, in which case any cyclical interpretation would obviously be weakened. In 1531 relations with Denmark were bad. In 1532 a revolt against the magistracy broke out at Brussels. As often happens in the sixteenth century, it began with violence against grain speculators.[10] The rapid spread of Anabaptism in 1533 was certainly not due to chance either, although grain prices fell considerably at the time. Similar considerations could be applied to the iconoclasts of 1566.

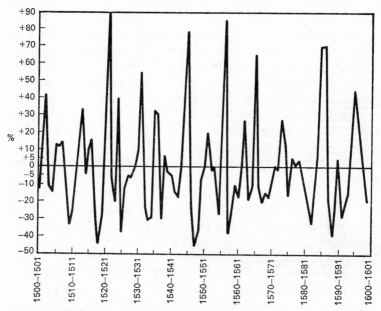

Figure 3 Cyclical price movement of wheat in Flanders.

It is well known that the Low Countries were not producing enough grain to meet their requirements. W. S. Unger,[11] basing his views on the tables of Nina Ellinger Bang, concludes that, on an average, during the period 1562–9, 47,224 loads (*last*) of rye and 4,233·3 loads (*last*) of wheat left the Baltic for the Low Countries each year. This represents about 100,000 barrels, some re-exported through Amsterdam, which was of ever-increasing importance as a redistribution centre. Let us say for the time being that the quantity remaining in the Low Countries was equivalent to 80,000 barrels. If we also go along with J. A. Van Houtte in putting the total population of the Low Countries at 1,800,000[12]—whereas Pirenne put it at 3,000,000—we should be quite safe in taking 2,000,000 as our basic figure, and thereby take in Artois, Lille, Douai and Orchies as well, which Van Houtte does not include. Yearly consumption per head was certainly 300 kgs.[13] In that case 600,000 barrels would have sufficed. If 80,000 were imported, this represented 13–14 per cent of the total, which was not so much for a country in which towns and population were, in those days, very dense.

The object of all the foregoing is simply to give an idea of relative importance, but it also helps us to see that there was scarcely any need to import when crops were good. When the harvest was only moderate some degree of rationing would have sufficed. Even so, the situation would then become precarious and the least threat of a bad harvest or a ban on shipping in the Sound would result in hoarding and speculation on the part of wholesalers. A slight shortage was enough to cause prices to rise sharply (according to the law of marginal utility). Hence the considerable differences from one year to the next during periods of crisis.

Nevertheless there seems to be little doubt that factors of the sort mentioned above, for all their relevance, remain external ones, and cannot account for movements of rising prices; the latter reflect truly cyclical processes. In fact a comparison with Henri Hauser's figures for Paris and even for Grenoble[14] shows that 1531, 1566 and 1587—with regard to Antwerp, we should bear in mind the closure of the Scheldt— were, for France too, typical years of crisis, although the external circumstances there were entirely different. True, the price movement may have been different in other areas, as is illustrated by Elsas's findings for southern Germany.[15] None the less, there is sufficient similarity between the Low Countries and France to show that external circumstances such as military action or the temporary closure of shipping routes do not provide an adequate explanation. Successive good and bad harvests, then as now, were probably experienced throughout the same wide regions and must have been the most important factor. The main effect of external circumstances was to intensify the already existing natural trends towards crisis.

Speculators naturally took advantage of all crises. They found this especially easy to do since bread cereals, as an essential product, underwent a sharper price increase in the sixteenth century than many other foodstuffs which were less vital to the mass of the population. If one takes into account only those variations which can be observed over very long periods or reasonably long ones, then this fact is not particularly apparent at first sight. For example, comparing the ten-yearly averages for 1500–10 with those for 1590–1600, it is evident that wheat in Flanders rose from index 100 to 595, oats to 520 or 550 according to the variety, butter to 700, but cheese only to 407. In Hainault between 1517–27 and 1567–77 wheat rose from index 100 to 245, butter to 291, eggs to 265, cured herrings to 138, salt to 341, soft soap to 245, olive oil to 212.[16]

Short-term movements are, in any case, much more revealing. In Flanders the 1521–2 year of crisis marks a 93 per cent increase over the preceding year in the price of wheat, only 31 per cent in the price of oats, and for butter 11 per cent, which increases so strikingly throughout the century, for cheese 26 per cent and for malt 77 per cent. At the same time, in Hainault, wheat increased by 115 per cent, but eggs by only 41 per cent, while butter went down 2·5 per cent; salt, although it was a product very prone to speculation, went down 17 per cent and olive oil 6·25 per cent. In 1531–2, another cyclical year of crisis, the contrast between rising cereal prices and the falling prices of other products is even more striking. In 1586–7, whereas cereals reached unprecedented prices, butter and cheese dropped, doubtless because demand centred on bread. So it is apparent that, in times of crisis, the movements of grain prices were much more violent than those of other products and so, considering the tremendous importance of grain as a basic foodstuff, one is entirely justified in determining periods of cyclical crisis by cereal price movements.

In addition to the above observations we must note that monthly differences in the price of cereals were particularly marked during years of crisis. Brussels provides us with very valuable material on this point through the *Cop du Pain* registers for the period 1568–9 to 1590–1 in the Central Archives of the Realm (*Archives générales du Royaume*).[17] They lead us to a number of interesting conclusions. During the crisis year 1585–6, the price per measure (*setier*) of rye in May was more than double the August price, i.e. at the beginning of the year following harvest. Much earlier, in November, the increase over the August price had already been 50 per cent, although supplies were far from exhausted. The situation was worse in 1586–7 since average prices exceeded those of the preceding year by about 50 per cent. Whereas rye cost 124·75 *patards* per measure (*setier*) in August 1586, it cost 244·25 in July 1587. The 1587 harvest was certainly a very good one, for although in August of that year a measure (*setier*) of rye was still fetching 90·25 *patards*, in January it fetched only 43·5, in May 21·2, and in July, just at the end of the harvest year, only 19, a low figure even in comparison to July prices throughout the period 1568–84.[18]

The most striking fact, though, is the extraordinary length of time— eight months—that elapsed before prices returned to a normal level. The lowest level, moreover, was reached just before harvest-time. It seems, in fact, that such movements cannot be accounted for by 'monopoly', that is, hoarding and speculation. We shall return to this question.

For the time being, we must point out once again that the phenom- enon of monthly differences in cereal prices, although always present, appears particularly marked during crisis years, as is shown by the series of graphs given in Fig. 5. These variations entail considerable changes in the weight of the loaf. We cannot here give a month-by- month account of such changes, but here is the yearly average weight, in grammes, of a rye loaf costing one *patard* at Brussels between 1568 and 1591:

1568–1569	*1,560*	1580–1581	*1,030*
1569–1570	*1,700*	1581–1582	*970*
1570–1571	*1,470*	1582–1583	*1,060*
1571–1572	*1,410*	1583–1584	*1,140*
1572–1573	*1,410*	1584–1585 (no cereals on the
1573–1574	*1,300*	market until April 1585)
1574–1575	*1,390*	1585–1586	*940*
1575–1576	*1,520*	1586–1587	*217*
1576–1577	*1,230*	1587–1588	*970*
1577–1578	*1,200*	1588–1589	*1,520*
1578–1579	*1,320*	1589–1590	*1,000*
1579–1580	*1,290*	1590–1591	*970*

Such a series of figures shows to what extent staple foods, principally rye bread, might, when available, fluctuate in price from one year to the next, and on some occasions not be available at all. These con- siderations will come into even sharper focus when wage movements have been examined. Moreover, the wide variations in the weight of the loaf, which clearly correspond to variations in cereal prices,[19] show once more that here we are in a field favourable to speculation.

The government of the day must have been convinced of this too, since it issued numerous regulations against hoarding. The government aimed especially at speculators (*recoupeurs*), who bought grain straight from the producer and kept it in store, or wine importers who sent

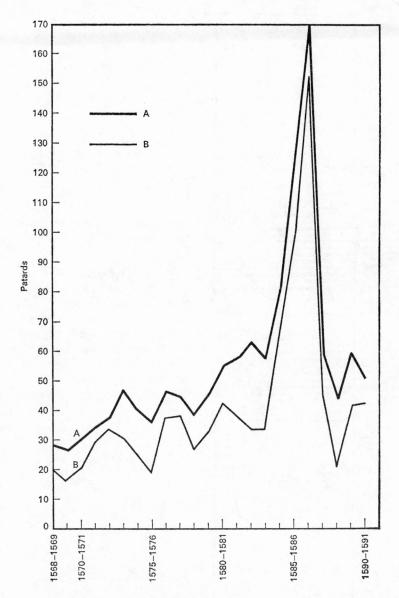

Figure 4 Price in *patards* of wheat (A) and rye (B) per measure (*setier*) at Brussels between 1568–9 and 1590–1.

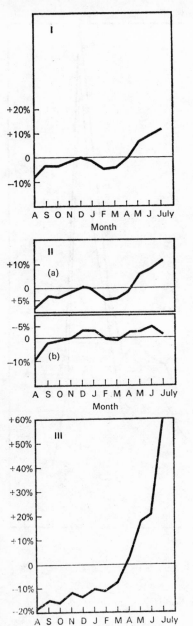

Figure 5 Percentage monthly variation from the average annual price (0=y-axis).

I. Average monthly variations for the years between 1568–9 and 1589–90.

II. Comparative diagrams: a. The average variations for all the years between 1568–9 and 1589–90; b. Average monthly variations between 1568–9 and 1589–90, not counting years of serious crisis.

III. Monthly variations during the 1586–7 cyclical year of crisis.

their agents to France to buy up wine in large quantities and let it out on to the market only in restricted amounts, so as to maintain the prices they had managed to impose. The swift development of commercial capitalism and the concentration of trade in the hands of wholesalers or importers brought about a weakening in the regulatory function exercised up till then by the old urban fairs and markets. These insti-

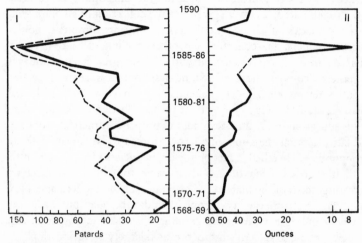

Figure 6 Comparative diagrams: I. Price (in *patards*) of wheat per *setier* (––––––––) and of rye per *setier* (————) at Brussels 1568–9 to 1590–1; II. Weight (in *ounces*) of rye bread costing 1 *patard*.

tutions, in the tradition of the mediaeval urban economy, existed to distribute supplies to towns, and to some extent, to the whole region. Capitalist merchants now endeavoured to avoid them in order to be free to stock-pile for their own profit. Such merchants also formed themselves into groups to control the circulation and distribution of goods and thus maintain high prices.[20] Regulations were issued time and again—a fact which tends to show the government's impotence. They state that growers may sell their cereals only at markets—aiming obviously at the speculators. Contracts on young wheat are forbidden. Grain, butter and cheese may not be hoarded by those who have 'large corporate accounts' (*grosses bourses ensemble*). In 1551, inspection of granaries was proposed for merchants hoarding Baltic grain.

Even so, all these political measures were somewhat ineffectual. Sometimes maximum prices were imposed; hardly anything ever

came of it. Much more often the measures adopted took the form of a
ban on exports of grain and other foodstuffs from the province or the
country as a whole—measures that recur throughout the *ancien régime*.
On other occasions attempts were made to maintain cereal supplies by
forbidding the brewing of high-density beers. Sometimes the town itself
might build up stocks of grain, so as to be able to sell bread cheaply to
the needy.[21] At Louvain and Vilvorde in 1521, the housewives gathered
in the streets and orders were given for 'the collection of all grain lying
in the granaries of abbeys, monasteries, convents, hospitals, nobles,
citizens, rentiers, tax-collectors and others holding wheat' ('recolle-
ment de tous les grains se trouvant dans les greniers des abbayes,
monastères, couvens, hostels Dieu, nobles, bourgeois, rentiers, censiers
et autres tenans bledz').[22] In general, as we have already said, such
measures did not go very far. A ruler such as Charles V was still bound
by his education to the mediaeval idea of proper commercial procedure
and fair prices; at the same time he was forced to be lenient with the
'monopolists'. He relied in fact on the big financiers to advance him the
funds he needed, even though these came too slowly to meet the
increasing needs of the State at the beginning of the modern age. Now
such financiers were the very people who did the hoarding, or at least
they were in league with the latter. Rather than take steps against them,
Charles V chose to stifle the disorders caused largely by their actions.

Certain ordinances inform us about these actions. That of 31 August
1556, for instance, forbids what it terms *setkoopen*.[23] This is what was
meant: a sum of money is advanced to a third party; a calculation is
made estimating the amount of grain the sum will buy at market prices,
at the time the loan is agreed; the debtor is pledged to repay the same
amount of grain at a time selected by the creditor; so the latter speculates on rising prices. If he himself is a merchant working on a fairly
large scale, obviously he is in a position to make the product scarce and
push up prices. Now 1556, the year in which the ordinance was made,
was in fact a cyclical year of crisis. So the situation was that that year
was particularly favourable to such speculation.

Moreover 1565–6 was a cyclical year of crisis combined with a
temporary closure of the Sound. High prices brought famine. The
masses became all the more receptive to Calvinist preaching, and in
August 1566 the iconoclast movement broke out. It is true that the
price of grain had dropped considerably between May and August.[24]
But the spirit of revolt had built up during the months of high prices.
When the Sound was reopened, stocks of grain had been brought on

to the market even before the first ships arrived from the Baltic. So it was patently obvious that the monopolists (*monopoleurs*) were not unaware of the hardships suffered by the people. Nor were the people under any illusions. At Ghent, revolt was, in the first place, aimed at grain merchants. At Antwerp, in September 1565, a granary belonging to one of the biggest merchants in the city, Pauwels van Dale—who was associated in 1564 with the powerful des Fourmestraux company at Lille—collapsed and spilled its wheat at the feet of the starving mob, and a riot broke out in consequence. At the end of the year 1565, the Lille merchants, des Fourmestraux and de Lobel, had already been accused of piling up huge quantities of cereals at Amsterdam and elsewhere in order to keep them off the market and so raise prices. The matter was hushed up, for Fourmestraux and Lobel knew how to cover themselves, and as a double precaution they were both zealous Calvinists.[25]

The people clearly hated the very idea of speculation and, rightly or wrongly, suspected monopolists of the most evil designs. In a play written by the Haarlem rhetorician, Lauris Jansz, they are accused of having themselves conspired to bring about the closing of the Sound. This play, intended for a popular audience, bears the revealing title *Van 't coren* (*Concerning Wheat*) and is dated 4 November 1565, a time when prices were at their highest. It describes the intrigues of two monopolists who try to make the maximum profit out of the distress of the times. It may well have been the action of Fourmestraux and Lobel that roused the author to write as he did. The virulence of the text shows how wrought up popular opinion had become.[26] We have other evidence too. On 4 December 1565 the secretary of the Privy Council wrote to Granvelle, saying that at Malines a number of houses belonging to grain merchants had been marked with blood. And he added, 'May God preserve us from all insurrections, for if the people were to rise in rebellion, I fear that religious matters would be mixed up in it' ('Dieu nous veulle garder de quelque grande sédicion, car si le peuple se haulsoit, je craindroie que le fait de la Religion y serait entremeslé').[27] And that was what actually happened some months later. On 12 May 1566, when the price of grain had already dropped following the reopening of the Sound, Morillon, the Provost, wrote to Granvelle:[28] 'If the high prices had continued ... everything would have fallen into confusion' ('Si la cherté heut continué ... tout fut allé en confusion'). But his optimism was premature. The confusion came in any case, in spite of falling prices. Thus Morillon, on 31

August 1566, i.e. after the iconoclast disorders, already felt anxious about the coming winter, even though it seemed likely to be better than the previous one. He feared especially that the thousands of workers in the Audenarde, Tournai, Valenciennes, Ath, Enghien and Nivelles textile industry, overcome with hunger, 'would take desperate action' ('ne jouent à la despérade').

If other proofs are required of the link between the iconoclast movement and the high price of grain, they are to be found in an account of the events that took place at Ghent, given by Marcus Van Vaernewyck, a Catholic citizen of some standing.[29] Vaernewyck must have known the grain business well for he held an important post in the Ghent market. He knew that merchants took steps to maintain high prices, and he says so. He notes that in August, soon after the harvest, prices once more showed a tendency to rise, though this tendency lasted only a short time. Nevertheless, in those unhappy times, when the people were suffering badly from poverty, and a few words could make them despair, it was enough to spark off a riot against grain merchants, among whom was the 'amman' himself. As the population became bolder with the new religion, some of the merchants were very nearly killed. To appease the malcontents, the magistrate announced that a decree was being prepared against the speculators (*recoupeurs*). And it was on the next day that the iconoclast movement broke out. We may wonder whether the religious direction of the agitation at the time did not in fact save many property-owners; we may be particularly entitled to do so, since, after the disorders, prisoners are said to have declared that they were sorry not to have gone for the coffers of the rich.[30] Of course there is no question here of explaining iconoclasm in terms of an over-simplified economic determinism, but the intention is to stress that it will no longer do to cut off religious or political aspects of sixteenth-century life from economic and social factors, as was done to an excessive degree in the last century, and as a certain number of out-of-date historians or enemies of truly human (and therefore complex) history still try to do now. It seems more and more certain that the poverty which periodically afflicted the lower classes drove them to expect an improvement in their situation from any new religion. Hence—at least as far as the masses were concerned—the rapid, almost unprecedented success of Calvinist preaching in 1565 and 1566.

In the eyes of contemporaries, including the government, monopolies were, I repeat, the main if not the only cause of high prices. It was not until 1568, when high prices had long been a universal fact of life, that

Jean Bodin suggested that increased stocks of money were the chief and almost the sole explanation.[31] For him, monopolies played only a secondary role. However, there is still one perplexing question for the present-day specialist in the history of prices, if Bodin's quantitative

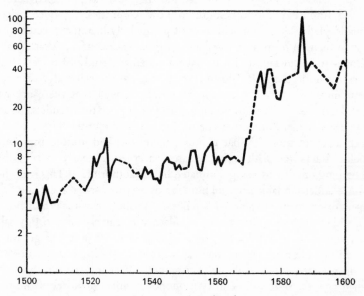

Figure 7 Price per barrel of salt in Hainault (in *livres*).

conception is accepted, or even if it is corrected on the basis of Irving Fisher's formula which also takes account of the volume of transactions (in fact rather difficult to measure in the sixteenth century[32]) and the velocity of circulation, which certainly increased during the sixteenth century because of the general employment of new methods of payment and credit. The constant increase in stocks of precious metals together with increased velocity of circulation may well explain the long-term tendency of prices to rise; but they do not account for the jagged appearance of most price curves—that is to say, they do not account for the sharpness of the shorter crisis movements. One has the distinct impression that, although the general rise may have been due largely to causes of a quantitative nature, it is not possible to account for short, sharp rises—precisely those which are felt most keenly by the greatest number—without taking the activity of the monopolists into account. This applies above all to prime essential products such as grain and salt. At the end of the century in Hainault, salt cost more than ten times more than at the beginning,[33] but precisely round 1568 its price curve remains relatively calm. When the Scheldt was closed in 1572 and Zeeland passed into the hands of the Prince of Orange, a sudden change took place. It was, in fact, in Zeeland that salt was processed before being imported into the southern Low Countries. At once prices quadrupled. Salt became a subject of particularly lucrative speculation. From then on no price curve had so capricious a course as that of salt. Goris—who, in fact, did not make a systematic study of prices—had already noticed this.[34] Grammaye, municipal secretary at Antwerp, announced in 1576, 'Everyone knows quite well that there are no products that undergo more rapid changes in price than crude salt and table salt, which sometimes rise in three or four months by 25, 30, 40 per cent and more.' What is more, merchants had noticed this even before the period with which we are concerned. As early as 1557 the hoarding of salt was being combated by the authorities.[35] This is all the more understandable since all households prepared salted meat and fish in autumn to meet their winter needs. A Ghent chronicle tells how, precisely in the year 1572, the populace was scarcely able to buy salt for this purpose any longer, because the price per sack had gone up from 1 or 2 florins to more than 12, as a result of the loss of Zeeland.[36]

In their conception of the possibilities offered by the economy of their age, the sixteenth-century monopolists differed entirely from the trusts and corporations of our time. While the latter aim to maintain long-term prices at as profitable a level as possible, avoiding any sudden change, sixteenth-century monopolist business seems to have been too spasmodic and intermittent to be able to proceed in this way. Monopolist business did not control prices, it disturbed them by pouncing on every short-term opportunity for speculation. The societies it formed were dissolved as soon as such ends had been attained.

However the idea of State-controlled monopolies effectively regulating price fluctuations was not foreign to the age. During the second half of the century, ingenious Italian adventurers such as Benevento, Schiappalaria and Baroncelli strove to have their schemes accepted by governments. An attempt to form a State-organized salt monopoly failed.[37] The irregular course of the price curve for this commodity, moreover, well illustrates the need. In 1561, Baroncelli proposed to create a State monopoly on imports and sales of wine from Poitou. Prices would be fixed and a share of the profits go to the State. But the State in the event preferred to avoid action and let the speculators carry on. It is obvious that the State could not or would not see that the Italian's scheme aimed at benefiting the consumer. Moreover, it must be said in defence of the authorities that in this case a luxury product was being dealt with in respect of which commercial monopoly never led to very pronounced short-term rises. The price of wine went up constantly from 1539 onwards, but it never doubled from one year to the next as grain and salt often did. Variations in price rarely exceeded 20 per cent. From 1576 onwards the price of Rhine wine and French wine increased very greatly but with hardly any convulsions. The annual rise and fall, noticeable in the late Middle Ages and during the first half of the sixteenth century, has disappeared. Only the buying power of money seems to fall continuously. At least, this is the case in the Low Countries. In the productive regions, years of good and bad harvests still contrast with one another in violent price variations.[38] This marked contrast between prices in the production area and prices in the consumer area is an obvious consequence of the development of commercial capitalism and the concentration of wholesale trade in the hands of an increasingly restricted number of firms.[39] Such business houses let only a small amount of wine at a time out on to the market and thus prevented demand falling beneath supply; thus high prices were maintained. At that time wines were drunk in the year of vintage or soon after. So profit was far greater after good harvests. But even when the wine harvest was less favourable, prices were not greatly increased. Wholesalers indeed knew full well that excessive raising of prices would limit demand for the luxury product they were selling. And they could not make good their losses by reducing the price of old wines, since they did not keep the produce of past harvests. Nevertheless the government issued ordinances against monopolies in this domain as well. They had no more effect than the tariffs that towns tried to impose.

Before we pass on to salaries, let us spend another moment considering prices expressed in terms of precious metals.

One may wonder whether the drop in buying-power was not due as much to faster circulation as to increase in stocks of precious metals. For, when it has been fully taken into account, was the influx from the New World, on which Hamilton lays such stress, really sufficient to meet the new needs of commerce in Western Europe? The 20–*patard* florin, the most commonly used coin in the Low Countries, continually lost in fine-weight, as J. Ruwet has shown.[40]

From 20·3967 grammes in 1507, it fell to 18·9088 in 1521, 18·008 in 1557, 17·188 in 1559, 14·544 in 1573 and 13·506 in 1575. It rose again to

15·126 in the following year, but then fell back to 13·506; then, in 1579, it dropped right down to 12·6058, sank even further to 11·458 in 1581 and went down to 9·5606 in 1612. Up to 1550 the decline is fairly slight, but between 1552 and 1581 the drop is 36·4 per cent. Taking the sixteenth century as a whole, we can say that prices expressed in precious metals are about 40 per cent below prices expressed in currency, and this does not take into account the difference between the precious metal rates officially laid down and the actual rates in practice, about which, generally speaking, we have no information. A drop in the intrinsic value of coinage acting in conjunction with the price rise was a phenomenon that was not restricted to the Low Countries alone. It has been observed elsewhere, in particular in France. Speaking of the Liège Region, M. Lejeune states that 'the debasement of coinage was less marked than the rise in price of foodstuffs'. 'These rising prices', he adds, 'clearly reflect the world-wide depreciation of money due to the arrival of American metal, but they also obey determining factors outside the field of money', which doubtless means that the determining factors referred to are not simply the result of an increase in stocks of precious metals. And M. Lejeune goes on, 'Whereas the Liège florin falls to half its former strength, a large basket (*panier*) of coal costs five times as much in 1600 as it did in 1550.' According to our knowledge of the extent of the depreciation of money, this could only be the result of a sharp increase in demand over supply. The same applies to munitions, for which there was a heavy demand from Spain.[41] Conclusion: it is quite clear that less and less could be bought for the same weight of pure bullion, but the drop in the buying-power of bullion is far less marked than the rise in price of foodstuffs. So the rudimentary quantitative explanation offered by Bodin is even more incomplete than one might think at first glance, and we have already noted that according to Fisher's formula, which is more sensitive to subtle differences, the most important factor for the sixteenth century was increased speed of circulation. Moreover, it seems to us that the quantitative theory, in whatever form it may appear, is not capable of providing a complete explanation of the price rise in the sixteenth century. As far as the second half of the century is concerned, one might even ask whether it was not the price movement, which, once under way, made it necessary to create additional currency.

As far as wages are concerned the traditional view is that they did not follow prices. M. Delatte has produced some figures for Hainault which seem to show that wages were increased threefold whereas prices increased fivefold, but these data are very incomplete. Even less credence should be given to a similar view, once expressed by Hector Denis on an almost non-existent basis.[42]

Decrees on wages, especially those of 1588, which we have studied elsewhere,[43] always propose reductions. In 1561 the States of Brabant decided to hold consultations with a view to bringing out a decree on wages, which had risen as a result of the 1556-7 cyclical crisis. 'Thus recognizing the rise of the said wages to have been caused chiefly by the high price of grain occurring in these years 1556 and 57' ('Cognoissans aussi la haulce desdits salaires principalement avoir esté introduicte par la grande chierté des graines qui fut ces années LVI and LVII'), runs an announcement by the Grand Council of Malines dated 6 February 1561. The point of view expressed at such deliberations is that of the property-owning class. Indeed the announcement we have just quoted states that everyone is 'oppressed and crushed by the huge, excessive wages and other benefits that the workers daily obtain . . . to the point of almost holding to ransom and oppressing their masters . . . by refusing to work, preferring to spend almost half their day in idleness, wretchedly spending their huge and unreasonable earnings in taverns and cabarets . . . by such means holding everyone in subjection' ('oppressé et foullé des grans et trop excessifs salaires et aultres advantaiges que les ouvriers practiquent journellement . . . jusques a quasi ranchonner et con-straingdre leurs maîtres . . . par non vouloir ouvrer, aymans mieulx passer quasi la moictié du temps en oysiveté et a malheureusement despendre en tavernes et cabaretz leurs grans et desraisonables gaiges . . . tenant par ce moyen tout le monde en leur subgection').[44] Yes indeed, unhappy rich men! And this point of view reappears at many other 'consultations' in the northern as well as in the southern Low Countries, including all sorts of considerations and information. The entire collection of material will be studied and published else-where.

If the study of prices is still in its infancy in Belgium, the study of wages is even less advanced. In order to give some idea of the move-ments to which wages are subject, we will consider their development in the town which, economically speaking, was the most important in the country, that is, Antwerp. Research at present in progress is based mainly on the accounts of the cathedral chapter and the Saint Elisabeth Hospital and on the archives of the Plantin press.

It seems that wages did not change at all during the second half of the fifteenth century. Between 1440 and 1513 there is no alteration. Change does not come in until the sixteenth century. It is impossible to study wages separately from prices. Fig. 8 compares the rise in wheat prices,[45]

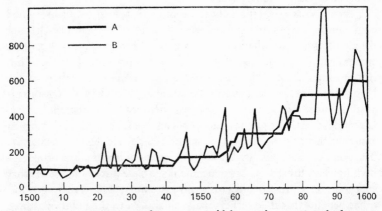

Figure 8 Comparative curves of stone-masons' labourers' wages A and wheat prices B (1491–1500 = 100).

during the whole period 1500–1600, with the rise in the wages earned by Antwerp stone-masons' labourers, on which we are well informed, men who may be considered as typical unskilled or only partially skilled workers. What strikes us immediately is that price movements stand out far more prominently than wages. The latter rise in regular steps and are only rarely subjected to backward movements. For the stone-mason we can make out seven successive steps with much shorter moments of increase intervening. Leaving out these periods of adjustment and increase, the longest of which is only six years, and taking the last decade of the fifteenth century as our measuring unit, the indices for prices and wages for the seven steps mentioned are as follows:

Years	Wages	Prices
1491–1500	100	100
1500–1513	100	92
1514–1520	114	102
1521–1542	128	156
1544–1556	171·5	199
1561–1574	300	290
1580–1592	514	515
1594–1600	600	596

Making wages for each period index 100, we obtain the result that average wheat prices for the periods considered amount to 92, 90, 122, 116, 97, 100 and 99. So price-wage relationships are favourable from 1500 to 1520, very unfavourable from 1521 to 1556, while between 1561 and 1600 an adjustment takes place resulting in a situation similar to the one obtaining at the close of the fifteenth century. This initial result topples traditional views.

During the second phase—which lasted thirty years—the price index fell below the wages index during six years only. The two increases of 1521 and 1543–4 did not make up for the cyclical rises of 1522 and 1545–6. The great price increase of 1531 was not met by any wages adjustment at all. The workman's situation was to change for the better only after the 1557–60 period of rising wages, following the sharp price rise of 1557, and the 1575–80 period, following the 1574 year of cyclical crisis. One final adjustment took place in 1594; it took the wages index up to 600. So the main period of adjustment comes between 1556 and 1580. Then the mason's labourer's wage moves up from 4 *patards* to 12, representing a 200-per-cent increase. This seems all the more surprising since it is in that very period that religious and political unrest broke out. So we must look into the matter a little more closely.

First we must note that in the years 1561 and 1574, during what was, from the political and religious point of view, a particularly difficult period, no wages adjustment took place, and that for building workers there was even a temporary drop of 25 per cent in 1567, that is to say, under the Duke of Alba's rule. True, this drop was well compensated for by an increase of 71 per cent for labourers and 66 per cent for master-artisans under the rule of the States.

But we must continue the analysis by bringing in other categories of workers. The table overleaf shows four levels of wages: 1530–5, 1550–1555, 1567–74 and 1595–1600. They correspond to stable plateaux, situated between the periods mentioned above in which increases occurred.

It seems that workers obtained an increase in their incomes sooner than their employers did.[46] Among masons, employed workers' wages were 46·5 per cent of their masters' wages in 1500, but 62·5 per cent in 1600. For rural workers the trend appears to be the same as that which we have observed for urban workers. Unfortunately we have little information on textile workers, except that they did not benefit from the great wages increase of 1557–61. For them the first significant increase is not until 1574. This is certainly of considerable importance in

Index of Wages 1491–1500=100

	1530–5	1550–5	1567–74	1595–1600
Masons:				
Master-masons	120	160	240	480
Journeymen	125	175	225	500
Labourers	128·5	171·5	300	600
Carpenters:				
Master-carpenters	120	180		560
Journeymen	125	175	300	500
				600 in 1601
Saw-hands	125	200	300	550
Tilers:				
Master-tilers	120	160		480
Journeymen	125		300	500
Thatchers:				
Town	125	150	200	450
Country	133·3			533
Pavers:				
Master-pavers	120	160		480
Journeymen	125	150	250	500
Labourers	128·5	171·5	257	428
Stone-cutters	114	171·5	286	515
Navvies	120	160	240	720
Gardeners	120	160	280	
Reapers	166			600
Threshers				
With meals	150			600
Without			350	700
Tedders (female)	133·3	166	233	533
Bakers (1526=100)		125		600

explaining their wholesale participation in movements of insurrection. Although cloth trimmers receive 5·5 *patards* a day in 1556 whereas masons' labourers get only 4, in 1564 they are still getting only 6 *patards* whereas most day-labourers earn more than 7. Not before the end of the century do textile workers catch up with the others.[47]

Now we must compare the above wages indices with a set of price indices for the same periods. These data, except those for wheat, have been obtained from the same sources as our data on wages.

The comparison shows how there was parallel development in the two fields, at least as far as bread-cereals were concerned, which, as

Price Indices 1491–1500=100

	1530–5	1550–5	1565–70	1595–1600
Wheat	119			526
(in Flanders)	118	210	288	614
Rye	158	208	246	707
Barley	147	206	259	610
Oats	126	153	170	515
Beans	98		161	314
Peas	130	179	185	466
Olive oil			288	740
Sugar candy				225
Salted herrings	144	152	266	570
Dried herrings	107	148	240	400
Vinegar	102		106	374
Pepper		158		315
Straw	156	167	325	450

we have already seen, rose far higher than many other foodstuffs. So it was, above all, the price of wheat and rye that determined income levels.

Even so we must not forget that between the prices and wages levels described there came periods of cyclical crisis during which wages remained far below prices. Three of these periods were not marked by even the slightest adjustment. From the social point of view, these were the most difficult periods of the century. They occurred in 1531–2, 1565–6 and especially 1586–7.

All the wages figures considered up till now have been for summer only. Winter wages were paid between 1 October and 1 March. During periods of adjustment a third type of wage generally appeared, which we may call spring or autumn wage, as the case may be. After periods of adjustment this intermediary wage became the winter wage and the summer wage was increased.

The winter wage fluctuated between 70 and 90 per cent of the summer wage and came closer and closer to it during the century. For masons' labourers it went up from 71 per cent of the summer salary in 1500 to 85·6 per cent in 1600; for master-masons, from 80 per cent to 83·3 per cent; for journeymen, from 75 per cent to 82 per cent. The result of all this was that during the course of the century winter wages show a much sharper rise than summer wages. Whereas summer wages for master-masons and masons' labourers show an increase of 480 and 600 per cent, winter wages rise by 500 and 720 per cent.

Of course these seasonal wages applied only to workers whose working-hours went according to the number of daylight hours, for instance building and agricultural workers. The situation is not the same in the textile industry. Cloth trimmers had to work at least twelve hours a day but were also able to do overtime, sometimes paid at the normal rate, sometimes at 110 and even up to 128 per cent of the normal rate. Workers in the tailoring trade had to work thirteen to fourteen hours in summer and ten to thirteen hours in winter. At midday there was an hour's pause. Work continued in the evening by candlelight. Agricultural workers sometimes worked on Sundays, for which their pay was 125 per cent of the normal. Such workers might receive meals. From the number of meals provided, food may be reckoned as 25 to 50 per cent of the wages. But here too we find that there was a gradual development in favour of the worker. By the end of the century 50-per-cent deductions for meals give way to deductions of one-third or a quarter. Moreover, salaries tend less and less to include any meals. On the land, farm-hands and serving-girls, if they are housed and fed, receive only 20 per cent of the wages day-workers are paid. Housing and food, then, were reckoned to be equivalent to four-fifths of the normal wage. In towns, apprentices, who were also housed and fed, generally received very low wages or even none at all.

Work performed in dangerous circumstances attracted special allowances. Stone-masons and tilers working on towers received danger-money that varied between 25 and 85 per cent. When workmen were laid off by their employers in winter they might receive compensation amounting to one week's pay.

The best way to work out the standard of living of manual workers in the sixteenth century is, obviously, to calculate the purchasing power of their daily income in terms of consumer goods; in other words, we must try to obtain an idea of actual income.

Here is a table for the mason's labourer in 1501–5 and in 1596–1600.

Purchasing Power of the Mason's Labourer's Daily Income (summer pay)

	1501–5	1596–1600
Rye bread	11·750 kg	9·870 kg
Wheat bread	5·850 kg	5·260 kg
Peas	7·28 l	12·45 l
Beans	6·64 l	15·2 l
Cheese	1·645 kg	2 kg
Pork		2·240 kg
Olive oil	0·970 l	1·035 l
Cured herrings	19 kg	29 kg
Rhine wine	1·47 l	1·1 l

The conclusion to be drawn from this seems to be that the workman's staple diet must have consisted of rye bread, peas and beans and probably cured herrings. Oil and wine were apparently ruled out. Furthermore, whereas the daily income for the years 1501–5 is equivalent to 11·750 kg of rye bread, the daily income for 1596–1600 can buy only 9·870 kg. True, the average increase in buying power with regard to vegetables is about 200 per cent. But we should need to know a lot more about the history of popular eating habits before we could interpret such figures correctly.

Obviously it is also necessary to take the average composition of a worker's family into account. Now this it seems must be estimated at five.[48] So the purchasing power calculated above applies to five people. It has been worked out on the basis of summer wages, and winter wages were 25 per cent less, so in view of this, and since no really serious crises occurred in the first five years of the century or in the last five, it is easy to see that if things were difficult enough for the head of a workman's family during the two periods studied, his position must have been very uncomfortable during crises. Moreover, this state of affairs must have persisted until the extensive drop in cereal prices in the present age.

So, from this analysis of data from Antwerp, we can conclude that if wages had in fact risen only 250 to 300 per cent during the course of the century, as is quite generally believed to be the case, the working class would have become extinct. Wages, then as always, must have followed the same course as prices. But even with a final increase coefficient ranging between 5 and 7, in practice wages at the end of the century do not come any nearer to adequately supporting a family than they did a hundred years earlier. It is easy to see how the worker—and the textile worker more than any other—was readily driven to riot in periods of crisis.

This explains why the wages tariffs ordered in decrees were not applied in practice. Whereas the 1588 decree[49] laid down 14 *patards* for master-masons, those employed by the Moretus[50] were getting 20 *patards* in 1592, and labourers were receiving 12 instead of 8. Moreover, neither the level nor the evolution of wages was uniform in the various regions, and the same is true of prices. This is very clearly shown by the records of the 1561 deliberations, to which we will return elsewhere. Nevertheless the number of those depending on public assistance must everywhere have been very high. We know, for instance, that at Louvain in 1546, a year in which a census of the poor was held, a nailsmith, a shoemaker's journeyman and a linen-weaver were earning between 1·5 and 2 *patards* a day.[51] At that time they could buy 5 or 6 kg of bread with such earnings. If they were married with two children, the ration was in itself very meagre and left nothing at all for other expenses. Without assistance, such households were faced with extinction. So it is apparent that wages simply must have followed prices, but without at all improving the worker's lot. This is sufficient to reveal the weakness of the traditional concept of the contrast between wage indices and price indices. On the other hand, however, we have seen that the evolution of wages includes quite lengthy static periods. It was in these that movements of discontent broke out; moreover, these did not very often have a specifically political or religious character, but had the more modern characteristics of strikes based on workers' demands.

Now we must sum up. We have seen the cyclical progress of price movements in the Low Countries in the sixteenth century, a progress determined above all by movements in cereal prices. Looking at things from another angle we have observed that the flow of precious metals from the New World was insufficient to prevent a decrease in the pure silver content of currency. Developments in methods of money payment, the progressive debasement of currency and the growth in speed of circulation offer a partial but not complete explanation of the long-term price rise.

In accounting for cyclical crises we felt it proper to give prominence to business speculation. But 'monopolies' do not govern price movements. It is truer to say that they disturb them for short spells, except where luxury articles are concerned (e.g. wine). 'Monopolies' give short-term movements their catastrophic abruptness. Indirectly they probably influence the overall movement too. After each upward spurt, although such rises are partly artificial, prices never come back to their pre-crisis level. Monopolies thus to a certain extent helped to intensify and speed up the long-term rise.

Otherwise, contrary to the traditional view, wages follow price movements and above all bread-cereal prices. Nevertheless, family income is inadequate. Even after adjustment and multiplication with high coefficients, wages at the end of the century leave the worker completely exposed to short-term cyclical fluctuations. It is the latter that act in conjunction with movements of religious, political and social unrest or at least have some connection with them.

Notes

1 *Documents pour servir à l'histoire des prix de 1381 à 1794* (Brussels, 1902, C.R.H.); supplementary note (C.R.H. *Bulletin*, vol LXXII, 1903).

2 'Prix et salaires en Hainault au XVIᵉ siècle', *Annales du cercle archéologique de Mons*, vol. 55, 1937–8, pp. 97–114.

3 J. Lejeune, *La Formation du capitalisme moderne dans la principauté de Liège au XVIᵉ siècle*, Liège, 1939; J. Ruwet, *L'Agriculture et les classes rurales au Pays de Herve sous l'ancien régime*, Liège, 1943. The latter work of course gives information on the seventeenth and eighteenth centuries. For the sixteenth century, see also general information given by J. A. Van Houtte in *Algemene Geschiedenis der Nederlanden*, vol. V, Utrecht, 1952, pp. 206–8.

4 Professor P. Harsin (Liège) is President, and Professor C. Verlinden (Ghent) is Secretary. Professors J. de Sturler and J. A. Van Houtte represent the Universities of Brussels and Louvain.

5 No other products are shown in periods of the same length.

6 The mobile averages curve is based on Van Houtte's tables except for the years 1581–4, for which Van Houtte gives identical figures—these have been corrected and related to the tempo of price movement in Hainault during

this period, as recorded by Delatte. See also the movement observed in the records of Brussels market prices for the *Cop du Pain* (1568–91) given below (Figure 4, p. 63). Thirteen-year series are used here; Labrousse also used thirteen-year units.

7 E. Labrousse, *Esquisse du mouvement des prix et des revenus en France au XVIIIe siècle*, Paris, 1933, pp. 137–56.

8 'Ta bellen van marktprijzen van granen te Utrecht in de jaren 1393 tot 1644', *Verh. kon. Acad. v. Wet. Amsterdam, Afd. Letterk., n.r.*, vol. III, no. 4, 1901.

9 Cf. above pp. 69, 72.

10 A. Henne, *Histoire du règne de Charles Quint en Belgique*, 10 vols, Brussels, 1858–60, vol. VI, p. 22 et seq.

11 *De Hollandse graanhandel en graanhandelspolitiek in de middeleeuwen*, III, '*De Duurtepolitiek': Bijlage* II: 'Statistiek van de uitvoer van graan uit de Oostzee 1562–1569', *De Economist*, 1916, pp. 461–507, 488.

12 *Algemene Geschiedenis der Nederlanden*, vol. IV, pp. 224–30.

13 As far as bread and beer were concerned. At the end of the eighteenth century, when the potato was already to some extent playing its part as a basic foodstuff, a daily bread ration of 1 kg was considered insufficient in the Herve region (cf. J. Ruwet, op.cit., pp. 264–5, no. 4).

14 *Recherches et documents sur l'histoire des prix en France de 1500 à 1800*, Paris, 1936, pp. 107 et seq., 316 et seq.

15 *Umriss einer Geschichte der Preise und Löhne in Deutschland*, vol. I, Leyden, 1936, *passim*.

16 Comparisons of this sort ought to be made on as wide a scale as possible so that we may obtain a better idea of the differences in rhythm between individual foodstuffs, regions and periods.

17 *Corps des métiers et serments.*

18 For the general movement of the price of wheat and rye per measure (*setier*) at Brussels during this period, see Figure 4 (p. 63).

19 See Figure 6.

20 Cf. J. A. Goris, *Étude sur les colonies marchandes méridionales à Anvers*, Louvain, 1925, p. 462 et seq.

21 W. S. Unger, op. cit., p. 489 et seq.

22 A. Henne, op. cit., vol. III, p. 17 et seq.

23 D. Graswinckel, *Placcaet-Boeck op't Stuck van de Lyf-Tocht*, Leyden, 1651, under the year 1556.

24 At Utrecht the drop was 23 per cent according to Sillem's tables.

25 E. Kuttner, *Het hongerjaar 1566*, Amsterdam, 1949, p. 218 et seq.

26 Ibid., p. 228 et seq.

27 *Correspondance de Granvelle*, ed. E. Pullet, vol. I, Brussels, 1877, p. 27.

28 Ibid., p. 245.

29 *Van die beroerlicke tijden in die Nederlanden en voornamelijk in Ghendt*

1566–1568, ed. F. Vanderhaeghen, Ghent, 1872, vol. I, p. 91 et seq.

30 Ibid., p. 245. Cf. a note by the great Florentine merchant G.-B. Guicciardini, 1564: '. . . molti sotto ombra di religione non cercano altro che mettere una voltasacco li richi e depredarli' ('Many under cover of religion intend nothing else but robbing the rich and putting them to the sack') (M. Battistini, 'Lettere, di Giovan Battista Guicciardini a Cosimo e Francesco De Medici', in *Bibliothèque de l'Inst. Hist. belge de Rome*, Brussels-Rome, 1949, p. 240).

31 H. Hauser, *La Vie chère au XVIe siècle. La réponse de Jean Bodin à M. de Malestroit*, Paris, 1932.

32 In the present state of research, we may even ask whether the sixteenth century as a whole is not characterized above all by the concentration of big business in the hands of a few, rather than by any growth in the total volume of transactions. In any case, the buying power of the mass of consumers did not increase. Cf. p. 73, above.

33 Figure 7 above.

34 Op. cit., p. 465.

35 K. Verhofstad, *De Regeering der Nederlanden in de jaren 1555–1559*, Nijmegen, 1937, p. 168.

36 Ph. de Kempenaere, *Vlaemsche kronyk of dagregister*, Ghent, 1839, p. 110.

37 On salt, cf. W. Brulez, candidate for the F.N.R.S. at the Modern History Seminar, University of Ghent: 'De zoutinvoer in de Nederlanden in de 16e eeuw' (*Tijdschrift voor Geschiedenis*, vol. 68, 1955).

38 E. Trocmé and M. Delafosse, *Le Commerce rochelais de la fin du XVe siècle au début du XVIIe*, Paris, 1952: curve no. XII, Price variation per barrel of wine leaving La Rochelle, 1536-1561 (*courbe XII, Variation du prix au tonneau de vin au départ de La Rochelle, 1536–1561*).

39 See J. Craeybeckx's book soon to appear in the same series.

40 Op. cit., p. 82.

41 Lejeune, op.cit., p. 196 et seq.

42 'Les Index-numbers au XVIe siècle en Flandre', *Annales de l'Institut des Sciences Sociales*, vol. VI, 1900.

43 C. Verlinden and his pupils, 'Twee documenten over prijzen en lonen voor Vlaanderen en Gent (1588)' (*Standen en Landen*, vol. IV, Louvain, 1952, pp. 105-33).

44 General Archives of the Realm, Brussels (Archives générales du Royaume à Bruxelles), État et Audience, 1095.

45 Rye prices would be more typical, but there are gaps in those available for Antwerp. However, the development of rye prices runs parallel to wheat, except that the latter is a little less prone to rise.

46 A. Wyffels made the same observation in his unpublished first-degree thesis on prices and wages in Flanders.

47 No need to stress that this evidence from Antwerp on cloth trimmers'

wages needs to be combined with similar information on textile workers in the main production centres.

48 E. Scholliers, 'De levensstandaard der arbeiders op het einde der 16ᵉ eeuw te Antwerpen', in *Tijdschrift voor Geschiedenis*, vol. 68, 1955.

49 Cf. C. Verlinden and pupils, 'Twee documenten. . . . '

50 Antwerp: Plantin Moretus Archives, Reg. 710. Similar findings for Flanders are contained in the thesis of A. Wyffels.

51 J. Cuvelier, 'Documents concernant la réforme de la bienfaisance à Louvain au XVIᵉ siècle', *B.C.R.H.*, vol. CV, Brussels, 1940, p. 37 et seq.

Six

Central Europe and the Sixteenth-
and Seventeenth-century Price Revolution*

Stanislas Hoszowski

1 *Introduction*

Since the appearance of Georg Wiebe's classic work on the sixteenth-
and seventeenth-century price revolution in 1895,[1] numerous works on
the same subject have been written in several countries, especially in
western and southern Europe. This predilection is easily explained—the
study of the history of prices started in western Europe and the price
revolution was particularly striking in countries on the Atlantic coast,
which, owing to their situation, were profoundly affected by the
invasion of American bullion. However, major changes in the evolution
and structure of prices in the sixteenth and seventeenth centuries can be
traced throughout the whole of Europe.

It is therefore necessary to study this phenomenon in central and
eastern Europe if we are to become properly acquainted with all the
various features of the rise and structure of prices in different countries in
the period. While any single part of Europe remains left out and while
the continent as a whole has not been the subject of systematic research
into these movements and their repercussions on the economic and
social life of each individual country, we shall not be in a position to
regard our knowledge of the sixteenth- and seventeenth-century price
revolution as adequate.

Our aim here is to consider central Europe, the area which stretches
from the Adriatic to the Baltic, in other words the lands at present

* Paper presented to the Stockholm International Congress on Historical Studies,
August 1960.

occupied by Yugoslavia, Austria, Hungary, Czechoslovakia and Poland. East of this area, Rumania and Bulgaria, which at that time were under Turkish domination, would be the province of a study of eastern Europe embracing Russian lands as well, i.e. the part of Europe that was most influenced by the Black Sea trade and by commerce over the vast regions under the control of the Tsars and the Turkish Sultans.

The zone between the Adriatic and the Baltic was divided by geographical or political factors into distinct regions and did not constitute an economic unity, though links between the regions were created by the regular exchange of products. From east and south, goods passed through Ragusa (Dubrovnik), Venice and Trieste on their way to the lands of southern Slavonia (Ljubljana, among others, in Slovenia) and north Hungary, Slovakia, Austria, Bohemia and Moravia; merchandise was transported over the Carpathians and the Sudeten Mountains on its way to Silesia and Poland. Silesia was the most important road intersection in the lands south and north of the Carpathians, for the area had political contacts with Austria and Bohemia, as well as ethnic and economic ties with Poland and the Baltic countries.

Any comparative study requires, first and foremost, an assessment of differences between periods and between regions or countries, as far as the extent and intensity of trade and price movements is concerned; it also requires an explanation of causes and consequences in social terms. Although no precise, complete history of prices is yet available for all of the countries of central Europe, it may be worth attempting without more ado a preliminary survey of the price revolution in the area as I have defined it above.

Czech historians have the honour of having been the first to work out price statistics for the past. The necessary impulses for an enquiry of this nature actually came from the 1873 World Exhibition at Vienna where material illustrating the history of prices was on display.[2] In conjunction with Vienna, the Prague Chamber of Commerce and Industry arranged an exhibit of statistical investigations into wages over the preceding centuries—it was the fruit of two years of research in archives. Several articles and an abundance of statistical material on the prices of various products and on prices and wages in Prague and Brno, and on several seignorial territories in every country from the sixteenth to the nineteenth century,[3] were thus gathered together, but they were not scientifically exploited subsequently.[4]

Not until after the last World War was there a perceptible renewal of interest in the history of prices in Czechoslovakia. The Czechoslovakian

History Seminar at the University of Prague and the Czechoslovakian History Society (Professor V. Husa and Professor J. Polišenský) undertook research into this aspect of their country's past. The quantitative material gathered still remains rather limited.[5] Some information regarding prices and wages may be found in the appendices of works on economic history.[6] In general, the figures cover only brief periods and a limited range of products.

The Vienna World Exhibition also evoked considerable interest in the history of prices in Austria. Professor Inama-Sternegg, following the initiative of the Prague Chamber of Commerce and Industry, presented the exhibition with statistics for prices in the Tyrol from the fourteenth to the nineteenth century,[7] and some years later published a treatise on the available sources.[8] From yet another standpoint, A. Luschin von Ebengreuth produced an article setting forth the aims and methods of such research in Austria.[9] But it was not until the period between the wars that systematic research was undertaken, by Professor Pribram's team under the auspices of the International Committee on the History of Prices. Precise statistics for prices in Vienna and a few small towns in the neighbourhood were then published, and they provided a good basis of quantitative fact on which more penetrating studies could be founded.[10]

The price revolution in Poland in the sixteenth and seventeenth centuries was dealt with by Professor A. Szelagowski in 1902 in a work that was essentially based on historical sources of a descriptive nature, quantitative data being very rare:[11] his thesis opened up broad horizons but remains only a prelude to the history of price movements. Systematic research began after the First World War on the initiative of the late Professor Bujak and continues today, following the formation of the International Committee on the History of Prices. Nine books on the history of prices in Poland appeared before the war and two others just after the war.[12] They contain very detailed statistics on prices in five important towns over a period stretching from the fifteenth century up to 1914.[13] Statistical material for the period covering the fifteenth and the first part of the sixteenth century is rather rare; it is much more plentiful for the next two centuries and entirely satisfactory for the nineteenth. Research is at present covering three more towns; a portion of the statistics obtained is already available to serve as the basis for a more detailed study.

As far as I know, even in recent times few historians have shown interest in the history of prices in the various regions of Yugoslavia. A few scattered notes appear in works on economic history and particularly in works on commercial and industrial history.[14] Dr S. Vilfan has begun a study of price movements in Ljubljana, the capital of Slovenia, in the sixteenth and seventeenth centuries.[15]

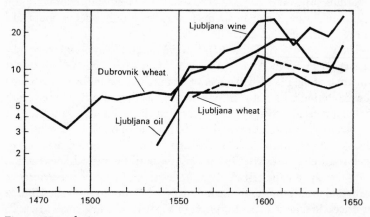

Figure 9 Yugoslavia.

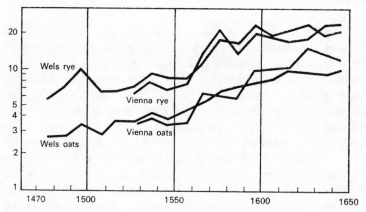

Figure 10 Austria.

Unfortunately, to the best of my knowledge the question has not yet been studied at all in relation to Hungary, Slovakia and Silesia, so these areas will not be included in the present article.

Finally, it must be said that, Austria apart, there is insufficient quantitative material to allow of any study in depth of the price revolution in central Europe[16] in the sixteenth and seventeenth centuries. The incomplete and scattered statistical evidence for Yugoslavia and Czechoslovakia can provide us only with a rough outline of such movements.

To present a better analysis of prices and their variations, reference will be made to diagrams drawn up in accordance with the data available for each country, those products being chosen for which the most ample and reliable evidence exists and which, at the same time, are most representative of the general movement.

2 Price movements 1500–1650

Quantitative material for Yugoslavia, although meagre, clearly shows that price levels changed little during the first half of the sixteenth century. They did not start to rise until after 1550, but they then increased very rapidly right up to the beginning of the seventeenth century. From then on stagnation and even a slight drop can be observed. There was no further rise until after 1640 (Fig. 9).

Prices of agricultural products in Austria follow a similar curve. Throughout the first half of the sixteenth century there is only one slight fluctuation—a temporary rise about 1530 and a fall about 1540. Then, in the second half of the sixteenth century, there is a sharp rise, which becomes considerably less steep in the first half of the seventeenth century (Fig. 10).

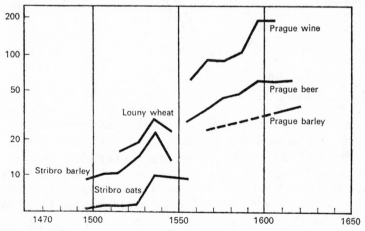

Figure 11 Bohemia.

The evidence for Czechoslovakia, though meagre and incomplete, shows the same trends. There was a very slight rise somewhat earlier, between 1521 and 1530, followed by another rise about 1540 and a drop about 1550. In the second half of the sixteenth century, the rise is very marked, becoming more gradual in the first two decades of the seventeenth century (Fig. 11).

Poland does not differ much from the countries already mentioned, but a steady rise in cereal prices had already set in during the third decade of the sixteenth century (Fig. 12).

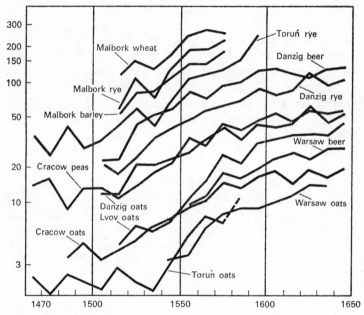

Figure 12 Poland.

So the general movement of prices in central Europe follows almost exactly the price revolution in western Europe[17]—a steady rise throughout the first half of the sixteenth century, a sudden climb during the second half, a slight tendency to rise in the first half of the seventeenth century. The only differences to be noted concern the starting date of the main steady rise in prices and the extent of this rise, in respect of certain products.

The important, enduring rise begins about 1550 in western Europe;

similarly at Dubrovnik and in Austria and Bohemia. On Polish territory, however, prices rose without a break from between 1521 and 1530 until 1550, when they had already reached a high level. The reason is that Poland was the greatest cereal exporter; the rise took place there before the invasion of American 'treasure' and the great upheavals which followed it throughout Europe (about 1550). Striking proof of this is given by the sudden rise recorded in the port of Gdańsk (Danzig), precisely where foreign orders for Polish cereals were felt most keenly, while at the same time the rise in prices of imported industrial products was very slight, precisely because of the constant rise in cereal prices and the accumulation of capital that resulted from payments in foreign currency.

3 Sharpness of the price rise

We have insufficient data to assess the detailed differences of price changes in the various central European countries in the sixteenth and seventeenth centuries and to compare the scale of the long-term movements of groups of products.

The sharpness of the rise in the different classes of goods varies from country to country. However, the prices of crops everywhere rise more than other prices,[18] followed closely by meat.[19] The very marked rise in cattle and meat prices in the port of Danzig is due to the heavy local demand as well as to the demand created by ships which were constantly increasing in number.

The sharpest rise recorded in the price of beef, in Austria and Bohemia, where it was dearer than anywhere else, shows that there was a considerable increase in demand, due not only to the increase in population but also to changes in diet.

Prices of building materials rose unequally, in some cases slowly, in others even faster than cattle prices, but all were less than the increases in the price of crops.[20] The variations in the price rises of certain materials show to what extent they were influenced by local conditions. For instance, the considerable rise in the cost of wood at Danzig is due to the growing export trade as well as to the ever-growing need for timber for local building and for the shipyards.

Manufactured goods take second place in this increase in prices,[21] since the price movement brought about by the importation of precious metals from America is here held in check by technical progress, which reduced basic costs in various ways. Price statistics for Austria and

Poland confirm the existence of considerable differences in this field. Central and western Europe experienced the same movements.

The information we have for Prague and for some other towns in Bohemia is not such as to enable us to assess with any accuracy the rise of prices there in the second half of the sixteenth century and the first half of the seventeenth. Nevertheless such significant evidence as there is for the period 1555–1618 confirms the Austrian and Polish picture—a particularly marked rise in agricultural prices, building materials in second place and increases in the price of manufactured articles occurring very much more slowly.[22] Statistics for Czechoslovakia seem to show that cattle prices rise more sharply than cereals, but the evidence is so thin that it cannot be accepted without reservations.

In the second half of the sixteenth century and at the beginning of the seventeenth, workmen's wages rose much more slowly than the prices of crops.[23] They appear rather to follow the course of meat prices, with corresponding increases, and this state of affairs continued throughout the first half of the seventeenth century, when the general curve for prices was flat or only slightly upward; there are even some examples of a downward movement. But if we take the general level of prices into account, we shall notice that, in central as in western Europe, actual wages kept well below the cost of living until the first half of the seventeenth century.

Some differences between the development of wages in Austria and Poland must be pointed out. In Austria, the increase was much slower during the second half of the sixteenth century (4% to 20%) whereas prices rose very sharply, and much faster, in the first half of the seventeenth century (22% to 70%), at a time when they were going through a period of less significant change. On the other hand, in Poland the rise in wages between 1550 and 1600 was very sharp (Cracow 77% to 80%; Lvov 67% to 145%; Danzig 81% to 150%), whereas during the first half of the seventeenth century, the wages curve was flat or even slightly downward (4% to 1%). It is hard to explain this phenomenon without more intensive research. As far as Austria is concerned, the devastation caused by the Thirty Years War may be the reason for this wage increase, whereas in Poland during the same period workers' earnings were restricted as a result of an economic recession.

A comparison between the rise in price of various categories of products and rises in wages would identify the particular characteristics of the economic situation of central European countries; but indices would have to be set up for each group of products and they would have to be calculated on a uniform scale. Results would be all the more interesting if the comparison were extended to west European countries. Unfortunately, such an enquiry could not be anywhere near exhaustive, for we simply lack the necessary statistics. All we can do, then, is to fall back on the case-study method, and restrict any comparisons to Poland and western Europe.

In Poland the rise in price of cereals was sharper than in western countries. Cereal exports via Danzig, from the second half of the fifteenth century onwards, consisting of locally grown produce, increased substantially when the rest of the country also began to supply cereals for export. Up till then, the demand for cereals in the distant coastal regions had been slight and local prices low. As soon as the trade route to Danzig had been set up and traffic along the Vistula had become regular, prices shot up, tending to equal those recorded at Danzig. Thus the rise in prices during the sixteenth century was sharpest in the provinces furthest from the Vistula and Danzig.

The prime cause of this rise in the price of cereals and other products was the influx of precious metals from the New World. The Polish market was flooded, and felt the after-effect more severely than France, Germany or England. There were two reasons—first, the very restricted development of monetary economy in Poland meant that agricultural produce represented a higher percentage of the total volume of the market than in western countries; second, the Polish economy was more deeply affected by the increasing quantity of currency in circulation, in so far as the need for payment did not grow proportionately. Manorial rent was paid in cash but wages were generally paid in kind, and exchange in kind was customary, while technical progress, which tends to bring manufacturing prices down and to increase consumption, was slower in Poland than in western countries.

4 Causes of the price revolution

Of the factors in the development of prices which favoured economic growth in the sixteenth and seventeenth centuries, some affected the whole of Europe, others only certain countries. It is not possible to draw up a complete list of these, nor to define the degree to which they affected price trends.

If we compare trends in prices in the sixteenth and seventeenth centuries in central Europe, with price movements in western Europe, we find that:

1 Up to the middle of the sixteenth century, the rise was slight and affected only foodstuffs.
2 From 1550 to the beginning of the seventeenth century, the rise represented a universal phenomenon and was everywhere of striking intensity.
3 The rise in price of agricultural produce and foodstuffs reached its peak in the second half of the sixteenth century.
4 Wages rose less than the prices of agricultural produce and foodstuffs throughout the period under study.

So the parallel development of prices throughout the whole of Europe was governed by the same factors. Taking the observations made by Jean Bodin as their basis, specialists in the history of prices have looked upon the influx of precious metals from America as the prime cause of the price revolution. But in the minds of these specialists other factors too have appeared to determine the rise in prices during the sixteenth and seventeenth centuries.

There is little doubt that inflation resulting from imports from the American mines brought about the devaluation of gold and silver currency in central Europe. But the situation was different in Austria, Bohemia and Poland. The first two of these had their own mines of precious metals, and their output had been constantly increasing between 1470 and 1510; after 1510 production went on expanding, although at a reduced pace, until 1530. Then it fell off, at first gradually, then sharply from 1560 onwards.[24] Although Austrian statistics for this period are very limited and data for Bohemia even more scattered and open to question, they show very clearly that there was a slight tendency on the part of the prices of agricultural produce to go up about the year 1500, in spite of a temporary fall. This rise may be due to accumulation of the output of central European mines, although there was at that time in Europe a considerable demand for precious metals and the output of these mines was relatively small compared to the huge imports of American 'treasure' during the second half of the sixteenth century.[25]

The situation was quite different in Poland, which produced practically no gold or silver. Gold in the form of ingots or coins entered the country only in answer to commercial needs—payment for cereals, timber and other produce exported through Danzig, and for livestock, salt, skins and fur sent to Silesia, Bohemia, Hungary and Austria. Accordingly, as cereal exports grew—from the beginning of the sixteenth century onwards—an increase in the price of agricultural produce became inevitable, and the rise in agricultural prices that took place in the second half of the sixteenth century is due to two factors which operated simultaneously and were parallel to one another—an increase in the amount of cereals exported and a drop in the value of precious metals resulting from the huge imports from America.

In Austria and Bohemia the great price upheaval of the second half of the sixteenth century continued until the beginning of the Thirty Years War and the monetary crisis of the 1620s. The collapse of currencies, the destruction caused by the war, the decrease in population and the economic crisis curtailed the rise, in spite of the ever-increasing influx of American silver ingots that continued until about 1660. From 1621 to 1650 the monetary value of prices hardly varied, and occasionally showed a downward tendency. It was the same in Poland—the great upheaval in prices ended about 1620, but for reasons of a different kind. Polish territory did not, at that time, suffer the ravages that occurred in the Hapsburg possessions in the wake of the Thirty Years War. Only one part of northern Poland, known as Royal Prussia, was devastated by the Swedish invasion that took place between 1626 and 1629, and this damaged the overseas trade of the port of Danzig. However, Poland had to meet heavy expenses in her wars with the Turks, Russians and Swedes. The amount of currency in circulation diminished. The monetary crisis of the 1620s affected Poland seriously and caused capital to flow out of the country. Prices were affected by the repercussions of an incipient economic recession, which, as is known, resulted from the system of demesne farming; this recession was evident in reduced industrial output, the slower development of urban society, a decline in the people's standard of living and, lastly, a drop in the amount of business conducted on the provincial markets. At the same time, the nobility, having grown rich from cereal exports, were buying increasing quantities of imported manufactured luxury goods. Commercial equilibrium was thus upset in spite of an increase in the export of cereals.[26] Finally, we must also take into account the downward tendency of European markets.

The second general factor that heavily influenced prices was the population growth that continued throughout the sixteenth century. But it is said to have helped to check the price rise in Austria and Bohemia during the Thirty Years War; historians differ as to the influence that population changes may have on prices.[27]

Changes in the total population figures seem to me of greater importance than changes in the actual structure of the population. Growth in urban population increases the need for agricultural produce and foodstuffs at the same time that it increases production of manufactured goods. Variations from one period to the next change the relationship between productive and unproductive elements at a rate that varies between town and country. This determines fluctuations in supply and demand and, consequently, the movement of prices. Absence of reliable statistics on the populations that witnessed the price revolution means that we cannot reach any valid conclusions on this point.

Other factors influencing the price revolution more decisively were economic prosperity (intensity of economic growth), production potential and, in particular, technical progress.

Economic growth was proceeding in all central European countries during the period of the price revolution, varying in intensity. It found expression in colonial expansion, increased agricultural production, growing exchange between town and country, the establishment of new craftsmen's and industrial workshops, and finally, foreign trade. All this went along with an increasing demand for raw materials, new technical equipment and manpower. Recruitment of new workers increased the need for foodstuffs, clothes and lodging. The rise in prices which was bound to result was checked in the case of certain articles by technical progress and a drop in manufacturing costs. The growth that took place in shipbuilding and means of navigation brought down transport costs and caused a general easing of the prices of all products. These factors were universal, creating differences in the amounts by which various products rose. The price increases in manufactured goods and imported products and those affected by hard currency were negligible in comparison with those of foodstuffs and building materials.

But there is a further problem—did the discovery of a new route to the Indies influence the price of spices and other goods coming from the Levant? These articles were still reaching southern Slav countries, Austria and Bohemia along the same routes as before. They were imported via the Mediterranean, passing through the towns of Italy, or via the west, passing through the commercial centres of Germany. Very little of this trade passed through Danzig and Polish territory. Prices of oriental produce thus remained under one single general influence in Europe—the drop in charges for sea transport between the Indies and

Europe. As for Poland, both the routes and the type of transport used for imports had changed. Up to the beginning of the sixteenth century Polish imports came up from the Black Sea or from the Mediterranean ports through Wallachia, Hungary, Austria and Bohemia, as well as from ports in the south or west and through Germany. In the sixteenth century these goods were imported by sea routes, through Danzig. So the price rise was less marked in respect of spices and oriental produce than in respect of other goods.

5 Effects of the price rise

During the price revolution wages fell behind, causing 'profit inflation'.[28] As has often been pointed out, increase in profits stimulated business and capital investment; it speeded up the development of capitalist forms of production and quickened the whole economy.

In western Europe the factors furthering these changes on the eve of the price revolution were as follows: the development of craftsmen's trades, urban and middle-class expansion, the availability of large amounts of capital for use in commercial exchange, and finally the partial collapse of the manorial system in agriculture (resulting in personal liberty for the peasants).

The new 'rising' class in western Europe, the middle class, took advantage of the 'profit inflation' to set up new workshops and develop overseas trade. As a result, internal markets expanded, as did production capacity; a capitalist economic structure developed. In central European countries, however, the opposite was the case—deeply rooted feudal structures were further reinforced by the new economic and social situation, and a whole series of restraints prevented development there of any economic expansion comparable to that of western Europe.

On the one hand, the flow of precious metal from America into Europe brought about a crisis in Austrian, Bohemian and Hungarian silver mining. The general rise in prices and the devaluation of precious metals meant that gold and silver mining were hardly profitable; competition from America thus seriously weakened the economy of these countries.

In addition, the price rise had repercussions on the social system, and on particular social classes. In Poland, landowners benefited most, while the disadvantages fell on the peasants and town-dwellers. The rise in cereal and food prices encouraged landowners to change feudal cash rents into labour rents. They created new demesnes, forcing their peasants to work on them unpaid. Minimal production costs and the huge profits to be derived from the new system encouraged the nobility to extend their estates at the expense of peasant farms and to exploit peasant labour on an ever-increasing scale. The nobility thus took over almost the entire cereal trade, cereals being the chief export, and through this increase in their income obtained decisive economic and social supremacy.

Peasants were unable to take full advantage of the rise in agricultural prices, because they had less land, and because they played only a very minor part in commercial transactions—a result of serfdom. Commercial monopolies set up by landowners even prevented the rural population from benefiting from any slight drop in price in industrial products and imported goods.

Nor was the Polish middle class able to use the profits which it had built up for the development of its industrial and commercial activities. It was handicapped by the political supremacy and the economic rivalry of the nobility. Business capital did not accumulate in Polish towns, as most business and the larger part of the export trade (cereals, timber and industrial raw materials) were in the hands of the nobility, exempt from customs duty, with very cheap means of transport (by river and peasants' carts). Large-scale cereal and timber exports transformed the Vistula into the main river route for Polish trade, and most export and import products were brought along it. This meant that a number of inland routes, to which several Polish towns owed their wealth, were abandoned. Such losses were not compensated for by a corresponding development of trade in the towns along the Vistula. Only a few cities in the northern provinces, Danzig, Elbag and Toruń, derived any profit from their intermediary role; the Polish nobility transported their agricultural and forestry produce to the latter towns by river and also made their purchases there of imported or locally manufactured goods. This type of economy, 'feudal' in character, killed business and crafts in the towns of the interior—they lost their manpower and their means of subsistence.

The continuing sharp rise in prices had yet another effect on social life. It made the cost of living very high, and this was deeply felt by a large part of the population. At meetings of the Diet there were constant complaints about exorbitant prices; these same grievances also found expression in political pamphlets. At the time, the reasons were not understood. The nobility blamed the merchants, accusing them of avarice and dishonesty. Middle-class writers attributed the deplorable situation to the commercial activities of the nobility. The poor cried out against the wastefulness and luxury of the nobility and the middle class. The outward flow of currency was also held to be responsible for the new state of affairs. State and local authorities legislated to check the rise—there were laws against luxury, official price schedules, regulations forbidding merchants to travel abroad or to take gold or currency out of the country. It all availed nothing; but such measures, which never affected the nobility, put another weapon in the hands of the ruling class for the subjection of the middle class and the peasantry. Price schedules covered industrial, hand-made and imported products, but did not touch prices of raw materials, crops or meat on local markets. In fact the prices policy protected manorial agriculture and took absolutely no account of crafts, business or industry in towns. These social and economic measures contributed to the decline of the Polish middle class.[29]

The same phenomena can be observed in Bohemia before the Thirty Years War. In that country, as in Poland, the nobility attempted—particularly during the period following the anti-Hapsburg revolt of 1547—not only to enserf the peasants, but also to engage in cereal trade and even to control certain branches of industry. Legislative measures taken against price rises in Bohemia were likewise detrimental to craftsmen and municipalities. During the second half of the sixteenth century, while prices were rising rapidly, the nobility played an even greater part in the cereal trade by buying in peasants' crops and forbidding their subjects to sell their crops in town markets.[30] The nobility alone sold wheat at local markets or exported it to Saxony.[31] Official price schedules handicapped the activity of urban craftsmen and allowed the nobility to develop production, on its own lands, of certain manufactured goods. This was especially striking in the brewing industry. The output of the breweries of landowners increased enormously and they became dangerous competitors for merchant-owned town breweries.

The price revolution thus expressed itself differently in western and central Europe. West European countries were more advanced in industry and capitalist economy, while central European countries were still dominated by agriculture and still had a very deeply rooted 'feudal' system. In the west, the price revolution accelerated economic growth and the development of capitalist economy. In central Europe, on the other hand, its effect was to strengthen and prolong the feudal system. Poland is a typical example of this—there, the price revolution of the sixteenth and seventeenth centuries resulted in the unilateral development of agriculture; it brought about an extension of the manorial system, encouraged the creation of 'the second serfdom' and impeded the development of industry and trade in towns, thus making the establishment of a home market especially difficult.

It is clear from this that the price revolution helped to emphasize the increasing contrast between the agricultural character of most central European countries and the commercial character of western Europe; it is a phenomenon which has been designated 'European economic dualism'. But, of course, it goes without saying that yet other factors affected the economic development of the sixteenth and seventeenth centuries.

Notes

1 *Zur Geschichte der Preisrevolution des XVI. und XVII. Jahrhunderts*, Leipzig, 1895.

2 The organizers of the World Exhibition defined their aims as follows: The prices of the more important products from the more important production areas must be displayed with illustrative samples. Prices should go back as far as possible and be tabled in the form of five-year averages. (E. Schebek.) See the following note.

3 Information on this material and certain facts about prices are given in the Exhibition Catalogue, prepared and published by E. Schebek, *Collectivausstellung von Beitragen zur Geschichte der Preise veranstaltet zur Weltausstellung 1873*, Vienna, don der Handels- und Gewerbekammer in Prag (Pavillo des Welthandels), Catalogue, Prague, 1873.

4 After the exhibition the manuscripts were placed in Prague University Library. The volumes devoted to prices in Prague itself are at present in the Historical Institute of the Academy of Sciences of Czechoslovakia in Prague. Essentially they cover the period ranging from about 1650 to 1870 and give practically no information about sixteenth-century prices. Data for Czech lands have already been expressed statistically by Austrian historians between the two wars, under the direction of Professor A. F. Pribram of Vienna. (See: A. F. Pribram, *Materialien zur Geschichte der Preise und Löhne in Oesterreich*, vol. I, Vienna, 1938, p. ix.) I have had no opportunity of looking up these statistics myself. As far as one can tell from

the contents of the Prague documents there seems little hope of finding in them any satisfactory information on the sixteenth century.

5 I wish here to express my deep gratitude to Professor Husa and his fellow-workers for their kindness in placing at my disposal various documents concerning prices at Děčín, Karlovy-Vary, Louny, Olomouc, Plzeň and Stříbro, as well as to Dr J. Novotný and Dr J. Jírasek, of Brno, for having allowed me to consult their notes on prices in Moravia.

6 Cf. J. Janáček, *Dějiny obchodu v předbělohorské Praze*, Prague, 1955.
J. Janáček, *Rudolfinské drahotní rady*, Prague, 1957. A. Míka, 'Nástin vyvoje cen zemědělskeho zboží v Čechach v letech 1424–1547', *Československý-Časopis Historický*, vol. VII, 1959, no. 3, pp. 545–71.
J. Novotný, 'Míry měna a ceny v urbarich a odhadech na Morave a ve Slezsku', *Slezský Sborník*, LVIII, 1960, pp. 89–111, 236–56.

7 E. Schebek, op. cit., p. 66, and T. K. Inama-Sternegg, *Beiträge zur Geschichte der Preise*, Vienna, 1873.

8 T. K. Inama-Sternegg, 'Die Quellen der historischen Preis-statistik', *Statistische Monatsschrift*, vol. XII, 1886.

9 A. Luschin von Ebengreuth, *Vorschläge und Erfordernisse für eine Geschichte der Preise und Löhne in Oesterreich*, Vienna, 1874.

10 A. F. Pribram, *Materialien zur Geschichte der Preise und Löhne in Oesterreich*, vol. I, Vienna, 1938.

11 *Pieniądz i przewrot cen w XVI i XVII wieku w Polsce* (*Money and the Price Revolution in Poland in the XVIth and XVIIth centuries*), Lvov, 1902.

12 *Badania z dziejów społecznych i gospodarczych* (*Social and Economic History Research*), F. Bujak, ed. vols. 4, 13, 14, 15, 16, 17, 21, 22, 24, 25, 37, Lvov, 1928–38, and Poznań, 1949–50.

13 A study of the history of prices in Wrocław is to follow, and there is the possibility of such studies being extended to cover other Silesian towns.

14 Jorjo Tadic, *Organizacija dubrowaczkog pomorstwa u XVI veku*, Belgrade, 1949.

15 My thanks are especially due to Dr Serges Vilfan, Director of the Ljubljana Municipal Archives, for allowing me to use the statistical results of his research on the history of prices in Ljubljana.

16 Dr M. J. Elsas, in his fundamental study of the history of prices in Germany (*Umriss einer Geschichte der Preise und Löhne in Deutschland vom ausgehenden Mittelalter bis zum Beginn des neunzehnten Jahrhunderts*, vols I–II, Leyden, 1936–49), includes Leipzig, but the price series he gives in this connection goes back only to 1570. It would be desirable to undertake a fresh study of prices before that date, even though there are few documents available.

17 See the diagram showing the curve of wheat prices in west European countries in W. Abel's work, *Agrarkrisen und Agrarkonjunktur in Mitteleuropa vom 13. bis zum 19. Jahrhundert*, Berlin, 1935.

18 The rise in price of agricultural products, 1551–1600, then 1601–50, may

be expressed in the following percentages: Dubrovnik, wheat 170% and 15%; millet seed 10% and [?]; Ljubljana, wheat 200% and 25%, olive oil 238% and 13%; Vienna, rye 178% and 25%, oats 150% and 28%; Wels, rye 145% and 6%, oats 104% and 22%; Cracow, oats 115% and 17%, peas 190% and 25%; Lvov, oats 392% and 32%; Warsaw, oats 171% and 60%, beer 213% and 23%; Danzig, oats 150% and 14%, rye 118% and 20%.

19 Prices of cattle, meat and dairy produce change as follows during the same periods: Ljubljana, meat 50% and 33%; Vienna, calves 44% and 70%, live bullocks 87% and 7%, beef 28% and 25%, fat 87% and 32%; Klosterneuburg, beef 45% and 3%; fat 124% and 6%; Cracow, beef 71% and 50%, butter 127% and 5%; Lvov, calves 102% and 23%, meat [?] and 1%; Warsaw, beef 103% and 20%; Danzig, bullocks 159% and 53%, calves 91% and 25%, beef 84% and 71%, pork 17% and 13%, tallow fat 143% and 17%, butter 54% and 37%.

20 The rise in prices between 1551 and 1600 and between 1601 and 1650 may be expressed as follows: Ljubljana, iron 142% and 0%; Vienna, lime 106% and 11%, bricks 44% and 62%, firewood 66% and 5%, timber 10% and 9%, nails 47% and 7%; Klosterneuburg, bricks 23% and 56%, timber 0% and 12%, nails 8% and 65%, timber (laths) from Cracow 65% and 21%, bricks 13% and 49%, iron 95% and 59%; nails 80% and 20%, batten nails 80% and 26%; Lvov, bricks 27% and 86%, iron 16% and 10%, nails 82% and 2%, timber 7% and 4%, firewood 80% and 46%; Warsaw, planks 53% and 75%, timber 70% and 90%, iron 49% and 43%, clout nails 84% and 96%, nails 47% and 106%, planks 103% and 79%.

21 The rise shows the following percentage increases: Vienna, paper 6% and 12%, soap 24% and 109%; Klosterneuburg, tallow 135% and 1%; Cracow, cotton cloth 9% and 12%, shoes 117% and 12%, cloth 46% and 13%; Lvov, paper 4% and 56%; Warsaw, paper 0% and 67%; Danzig, paper 20% and 49%.

22 Prices in the period 1601–10 were higher than in the period 1561–70, as is shown by the following figures: beer 74%, wine 21%, rye 29%, barley 32%, bullocks 307%, cows 165%, bricks 25%, timber 65%, nails 47%, carpenter 24%, apprentice carpenter 121%, journeyman 44%. These figures would have been much higher if they had been compared with prices from the end of the first half of the sixteenth century, as the two decades 1551–60 and 1561–70 saw very great rises.

23 Percentage rise in wages: Vienna, stonemason's apprentice 7% and 43%, carpenter's apprentice 17% and 22%, stonemason's mate 14% and 47%, carpenter's mate 16% and 42%; Klosterneuburg, stonemason's apprentice 4% and 70%, carpenter's apprentice 20% and 40%; Cracow, stonemason's apprentice 88% and 3%, carpenter's apprentice 77% and 5%, journeyman 80% and 11%; Lvov, stonemason's apprentice 145% and 10%, carpenter's

apprentice 67% and 10%, journeyman 76% and 38%; Warsaw, journeyman 55% and 11%; Danzig, stonemason's apprentice 150% and 0%, carpenter's apprentice 81% and 1%, journeyman 41% and 52%.

24 John U. Nef, 'Silver Production in Central Europe', *Journal of Political Economy*, XLIX, 1941, p. 590.

25 The total silver production of Africa and Europe about 1540 was 600 quintals a year, whereas the output of American mines in the second half of the sixteenth century was more than 3,000 quintals a year.

26 See S. Hoszowski, 'The Polish Baltic Trade in the 15th-18th Centuries', in *International Congress of Historical Sciences in Stockholm*, Warsaw, 1960, pp. 123-5.

27 See W. C. Robinson's discussion of this question: 'Money, Population and Economic Change in Late Medieval Europe'; M. M. Postan, in the *Economic History Review*, vol. XII, no. 1, August 1959, pp. 63-82. M. J. Elsas attributes variations in prices in Germany in the sixteenth and seventeenth centuries to changes in population (*Umriss einer Geschichte der Preise und Löhne in Deutschland*, vols I-II, Leyden, 1936-49).

28 See E. J. Hamilton, 'Prices as a Factor in Business Growth', *Journal of Economic History*, vol. XII, 1952, no. 4, pp. 325-49.

29 See S. Hoszowski, 'The Revolution of Prices in Poland in the 16th and 17th Centuries', *Acta Poloniae Historica*, vol. 2, Warsaw, 1959, pp. 7-16.

30 J. Janáček, *Rudolfinské drahotní rady*, Prague, 1957, pp. 26-7.

31 V. Sadova, 'Böhmisches Getreide auf dem sachsischen Markt am Ende des 16. und in der ersten Hälfte des 17. Jahrhunderts. Aus 500 Jahren deutsch-tschechoslovakischer Geschichte', Berlin, 1958, pp. 79-97.

Seven

Movements of Expansion in Europe in the Sixteenth and Seventeenth Centuries

Marian Małowist

These lines do not result from systematic or prolonged study; they aim rather to offer a few considerations and a valid starting-point for a general discussion of certain economic and social phenomena common to several European countries in the late Middle Ages and at the beginning of the modern era. I refer to those great movements of expansion which from the fifteenth century onwards preceded the long crisis, marked by widespread economic and social depression that set in, for certain regions of the continent, in the mid-sixteenth century. The period in question is not simply one of stagnation, for it saw important social and economic changes. I have for example endeavoured to show that a 'democratization' (if I may coin the phrase) of large-scale international commerce took place in the fourteenth and fifteenth centuries, particularly in the cloth trade, when textiles of average and even mediocre quality appeared on the international market in large quantities, especially in trade between the Low Countries and central, eastern and south-west Europe. From the fifteenth century onwards we observe a growth in the volume of trade in cereals and timber between the Baltic and the west. Spanish wool consolidated its position on the markets of Italy and the Low Countries and even reached England, which was itself an important producer of various qualities of wool. All these goods had increased in importance in international commerce despite the high cost of transport and the general decline in population.

From the social point of view, we might speak of a relative broadening of the field of mercantile activity. The social groups which were hardly involved in commerce in the thirteenth century became consumers of manufactured products: this led to the emancipation of the better-off peasants and the development of rural industries. Numerous peasants began to engage in textile manufacture, forsaking agriculture where the latter made only a meagre living possible. Similarly, during this period there was a relative expansion of the groups obliged to buy their food and ordinary necessities; this was followed by an acceleration of the division of labour, possibly because the former ruling classes were becoming poorer, while the poor were gaining ground. In the same context, we should remember the fall in the value of money incomes and the accompanying rise in the cost of labour. Nobles, clergy and the State suffered the effects of a general depreciation of currency; on the other hand, a large part of the peasant and town population improved its standard of living. This dramatic situation resulted in attempts at 'refeudalization' on the part of the nobility, and those cruel struggles between noble and peasant which fifteenth-century history records so abundantly (in the west as well as in Scandinavia).

Some historians see a connection between the great wars of the fourteenth and fifteenth centuries (including the French expedition to Italy) and the reduction of the nobles' revenues. Perhaps we should also include here the reappearance of lawlessness on the part of the nobles in all western countries, even in Scandinavia and, to a lesser extent, in Slav countries. Is it not also possible that the beginnings of the great movements of expansion of the fifteenth and even the fourteenth century (especially the colonization of the Atlantic islands) belong to the same group of events and were due to identical causes? The first signs of eastward expansion and the attempt by the Danish and German nobility to conquer Sweden might be considered from this same point of view. The latter enterprise, known under the title of the Unification of the Kingdoms of the North, was preceded by the invasion of Sweden on the part of the nobles of North Germany, who soon proved too weak to hold a prey that had been very easy to snatch.

In connection with the economic depression of the fourteenth and fifteenth centuries, attention has been drawn to the 'gangsterism' of the English nobility. Professor M. Postan explains this phenomenon in the fifteenth century by the drop in the English nobility's revenues and the tremendous difficulties in the way of any attempt to reorganize economic life. It is my view that the phenomenon was extremely widespread and constituted one of the most important aspects of the activity of the nobility in numerous European countries in the fourteenth and fifteenth centuries. Such activity manifested itself in even more violent efforts on the part of various groups of nobles to conquer new territories or gain political power and access to State revenues. This tendency stands out clearly in the fourteenth and fifteenth centuries, in Scandinavia and Denmark for instance, as well as in England. In Germany, the nobility's banditry, known as 'Raubrittertum', reached its peak in the fourteenth century and the beginning of the fifteenth. It may prove possible to observe something analogous in Spain. There are similar symptoms in Poland and Hungary as well, although for these two countries this was more a period of economic and political consolidation, and outbreaks of lawlessness on the part of the nobles were less violent than in western Europe. In fact, symptoms of the economic crisis facing the fourteenth-century nobility appeared in Poland and Hungary only after a certain lapse of time and they were, moreover, in my view, much weaker than in the west. And in the end this ensured for the Polish and Hungarian nobility a better situation than that of the ruling classes of western Europe. In eastern Germany, as well as in Poland, attempts to reorganize the nobility's livelihood, first at the expense of the peasants, then at the expense of the town-dwellers, can be noted as early as the fifteenth century; this helped to reduce 'gangsterism' on the part of the nobility. Being perhaps a matter of less urgency than elsewhere, in Poland the transformation of the nobility's means of livelihood went hand in hand with an extension of its economic activity to previously unexploited territories.

This set of facts prompts me to ask the following question: would it not be worth examining from this point of view the vast overseas expansion of the peoples of the Iberian peninsula that began in the fourteenth century and went on particularly in the fifteenth century, in order to establish whether this too was not, to a certain extent, the result of a depression in rural economy and a sudden drop in the nobility's revenues?

The overseas expansion of Portugal and Spain has long been the subject of unceasing detailed research. The commercial aspect of these conquests has frequently been examined and the effect of the Great Discoveries on European monetary conditions has also been clearly defined. Numerous books and articles, some excellent, have dealt with the ideological aspects of this vast colonizing movement. But it seems to me that our knowledge is less satisfactory when we come to ask what social groups were involved in such overseas expansion, especially in the fifteenth century and at the beginning of the sixteenth, and what the factors were impelling them to take part.

I shall devote myself solely to the aspect of these problems present in central and eastern Europe; but I shall be looking for facts likely to throw light on phenomena occurring in the north-west part of our continent as well.

Let us recall that it was more or less in this very period that vast migratory movements were beginning in central and eastern Europe. In Poland such movements affected territories of rather limited area, despite the fact that by the beginning of the seventeenth century they had brought the Polish nobility right up to the northern regions of the State of Russia. An observation recently made by Professor W. Czapliński is worth mentioning here: at the very moment when Polish eastward expansion reached its peak, contemporary politicians were comparing it to the conquest of the West Indies by the Spanish and Portuguese. They may indeed have been partly right; at that time, the conquest of Moscow (actually of very short duration) had been achieved not by the Polish State, but by the great Polish and Lithuanian lords aided by the lesser nobility who were dependent on them; there is no question here of political plans being laid by the State; these were economic enterprises resulting in the seizure of new territories to secure new sources of income. The Polish State took control of the operation rather late in the day—and in any case it was doomed to failure. Analogous phenomena, on a much smaller scale, occurred in Poland as early as the middle of the sixteenth century or thereabouts, when various Polish magnates attempted, once more on their own account, to conquer certain Rumanian territories, and thereby provoked a conflict between the Polish government and that of the Sultan despite the open disapproval of the vast majority of the Polish nation. Polish colonization also moved continuously eastwards in a less dramatic manner, towards the vast regions of the Ukraine, and northwards, towards White Russia and Livonia; at the same time settlers from Polish Mazovia began the intensive colonization of the great forests of East Prussia.

True, ideological problems here take a different form from those applicable to the Iberian peninsula. In the fifteenth and especially in the sixteenth century, it is hard to see any explosions of Catholic faith capable of inciting the Polish population to fight against Turkish Islam or the Russian Schismatics. The period was characterized rather by relative religious tolerance. It is only in the last quarter of the sixteenth century that Polish Catholics adopted war-like attitudes, and these were directed solely against the Reformation. The myth of Poland as the bulwark of Christianity—'antemurale Christianitatis'— grew in the seventeenth century during the defensive struggles with Russia, Turkey and Sweden.

Persuaded of the undoubted value of the comparative method, we wish to focus attention on the colonization of the northern territories of Russia (beginning in the fifteenth century, towards the end of the Novgorod Republic) and on subsequent conquests and colonization on the part of the State of Muscovy in southern Russia and Siberia.

Swedish, German and Polish historians have given much attention to the question of Swedish expansion in the second half of the sixteenth and the first half of the seventeenth century. Their research has, however, concentrated too narrowly on political problems. Although events occurring after the great transoceanic movements play a role here, perhaps it is worth dwelling on certain other aspects of Swedish domination of the Baltic. In fact the initially modest beginnings of Swedish expansion also belong to the fifteenth century. Furthermore, Sweden in the fifteenth and sixteenth centuries was economically a very backward country, not only in comparison with western Europe, but even with eastern Germany and Poland. In fact it seems that certain very interesting social problems inherent in Swedish expansion have not been truly acknowledged, even by Swedish scholars. In this connection we must recognize that the position of Swedish merchants in no way accounts for Sweden's aggression against her neighbours, since these same merchants drew but slight profit from Swedish conquests and at times even tried to oppose expansion, seeing it rather as a cause of ever-increasing taxation.

However, the group that firmly supported a policy of expansion was the aristocracy or nobility, which found it impossible to increase its very limited income by other means. This group supported expansion at the cost of a strong, well organized peasantry. Conquests and the administration of conquered territories in fact offered vast new sources of revenue first and foremost to the great lords and nobility. Expansion also put an end to the struggles between various groups of aristocrats, and between nobles and peasants—long-standing, enduring, endemic struggles that lasted in Sweden throughout the second half of the sixteenth century.

I add that it would be of the greatest interest to analyse Turkish expansion in the fifteenth and sixteenth centuries from the social point of view, but in the views of the present state of research the undertaking is inconceivable. In any case, we must agree that from the fourteenth century onwards numerous countries in south-west and eastern Europe —we should call them rather under-developed countries—went through a period of large-scale territorial expansion and attempted to create vast empires; but because of their economic weakness these empires were exploited by other more highly developed countries or even by internal opposition groups. It is only towards the end of the sixteenth century that the most highly developed countries in Europe, economically speaking, took part in the movement of expansion: they were Holland, England and France, all of which, even then, already had sufficiently strong economic and political systems. Dutch and English expansion, and French expansion too, which was far less extensive than the others, had new causes; they were no longer the same as those that had led to the great Spanish and Portuguese colonial movement of the fifteenth and sixteenth centuries, or the less spectacular but none the less unrelenting eastward Polish movement, or the Russian conquests in Europe and northern Asia, or even the impulsive well-organized Swedish offensive, which, though short, spread throughout the Baltic.

Much attention has been given to the commercial aspect of these expansions. Certain works have thrown light, at least partially, on the part played by the great commercial and banking houses in the exploitation of the Spanish and Portuguese overseas territories, though the subject is far from exhausted. In this respect Werner's article,[1] published in the *Vierteljahrschrift für Sozial- und Wirtschaftsgeschichte*, is of considerable interest. The author describes the role played by capital investment in commerce and the exploitation of mines in the New World, such investment being carried out not only by the richer financiers but also by merchants and nobles. Research carried out by Attman[2] in northern Europe has clarified the commercial aspects of the expansionist policy pursued by the Swedes in Livonia and Russia in the second half of the sixteenth century. Research done by a Polish historian, A. Szelagowski, had a similar object. The results of such research obviously cannot be compared with those obtained in recent years by modern French, English or American historiography. I have in mind the works of Hinton[3] and the particularly interesting book by Supple,[4] devoted to the commercial expansion of England in the Baltic in the sixteenth and first half of the seventeenth centuries, though I regret that

English-speaking historians have—altogether too perfunctorily, if I may say so—ignored the sources and conclusions of the research done by east European scholars. It is a pity, too, that up till now they have not given serious consideration to Scottish expansion in the Baltic regions: from the fifteenth century onwards this constituted a wholesale infiltration which, whatever else it did, tightened the economic links between the British Isles and the countries of eastern and northern Europe.

During recent years historians have attributed ever-increasing importance to the demographic factor; it is even looked upon as one of the most important stimuli to economic expansion. Thus Pierre Vilar,[5] and more recently Elliott,[6] have drawn attention to the population growth in Castile during the period preceding the Great Discoveries and throughout their duration—that is, during the second half of the fifteenth century. Boxer,[7] too, points out quite rightly that the easy victory won by the Dutch over the Portuguese in Africa and the Far East at the beginning of the seventeenth century can be explained by the fact that the Dutch were able to mobilize part of the population of Germany as well as that of their own new State. Polish sources for the second half of the sixteenth and for the seventeenth century show that the central and western regions of the Polish State in the sixteenth century were much more densely populated than in the seventeenth; they also show that the population of Mazovia was the densest of all, and this explains why the greatest outflow was to the east and north. Soviet scholars think that by the fourteenth and fifteenth centuries Russia had overcome the effects of the devastation wrought there by the Tartars, and that a great increase in the population of central Russia and the north-west took place, continuing until the end of the sixteenth century. Thence the population flowed back to the south and south-east. This demographic factor is less in evidence in Sweden (and Finland), which was sparsely populated in comparison to the other Baltic countries.

But, in order to appreciate the true importance of the demographic factor, we must take other circumstances into account. An English historian recently wrote that in order to analyse economic life in Europe at the turning-point between the Middle Ages and modern times we should bear in mind the present situation of under-developed countries. Although this approach can lead to dangerous simplifications, it seems to contain a grain of truth. For instance, it is well known that in countries now termed 'under-developed', rapid growth of population is not always favourable to development. The decisive element in such cases is whether the social structure favours or hinders economic progress. In certain social situations, population growth is hostile to economic development and makes the condition of the people intolerable; it is then that the most energetic among them seek their salvation in emigration, with all its dangers. The countries of eastern Europe had experience of this, not only at the end of the Middle Ages, but in the nineteenth and at the beginning of the twentieth century as well.

In certain situations men, however much attracted to local traditions and a certain way of life, decide to emigrate to distant countries; they show tireless energy and great courage in creating new and better living conditions. This fact throws a certain light on the problem of the migrations and great colonial conquests that took place from the fifteenth century to the seventeenth.

We admire the courage and perseverance of the Spanish and Portuguese 'conquistadores', even if their avarice and cruelty often rouse our anger. Numerous Polish and Russian historians and other writers have described with great feeling the life of the settlers in the Ukraine and in south Russia, where they were constantly exposed to attacks from the Tartars, yet obstinately continued their work of colonization. Difficult economic conditions and certain social situations hostile to economic progress seem thus to create conditions favourable to even the most hazardous emigration. It is obvious that external conditions may have facilitated such emigration at the end of the Middle Ages—and chief among these conditions was the existence of vacant land. Without denying the immense importance of the demographic factor in these great colonizing movements of the fifteenth and sixteenth centuries, it is right to draw attention to the social and economic conditions which, given the help of certain external circumstances, also release immense sources of energy; growth in population, moreover, may have even aggravated general economic stagnation.

It is possible and legitimate to object that there is scarcely any justification for drawing a comparison between lands as different as east European territories and the regions of the Iberian peninsula. Even so . . . what is needed simply is a definition of the extent to which social conditions in Poland and her neighbours in the fifteenth and sixteenth centuries exercised an influence on economic expansion within national boundaries and beyond them; and an account of the influence of such structures on the political forms and the aims of expansion.

Marian Małowist

Notes

1 G. Werner, 'Europäisches Kapital in ibero-amerikanischen Montanunternehmungen des 16. Jahrh.', *V.S.W.G.*, 48, 1961, 1.
2 A. Attman, *Den ryska marknaden i 1500 talets Baltiska politik 1558–1595*, Lund, 1944.
3 R. W. K. Hinton, *The Eastland Trade and the Common Weal in the XVIIth Century*, Cambridge, 1959.
4 B. E. Supple, *Commercial Crisis and Change in England, 1600–1642*, Cambridge, 1959.
5 P. Vilar, 'Le temps de Quichotte', *Europe*, XXXIV, 1956; also 'Le déclin du Bas Moyen-Age', *Estudios de Historia Moderna*, VI, 1956–9.
6 J. Elliott, 'The Decline of Spain', *Past and Present*, 20, 1961.
7 C. R. Boxer, *The Portuguese in the East, 1500–1800*, and *Portugal and Brazil*, Oxford, 1953.

Eight

Sixteenth-century Hungary: Commercial Activity and Market Production by the Nobles

Z. P. Pach

About the middle of the sixteenth century agriculture in Hungary was beginning to catch up with that of western countries. What then were the salient features of Hungarian farming at that time?

The feudal system of land ownership was characterized by the predominance of peasant tenure in relation to seignorial demesnes. The large seignorial estate rested on a foundation of feudal revenues rather than a system of large-scale directly-managed farming. Of the two forms of feudal rent not paid in money—corvee and tithes—it was the latter which was still widespread, while the corvee had become much less usual. The cash payment of rent had developed considerably not only in small towns, which had become more densely populated and were generally further advanced, but also in small villages. As for the peasant, although he had already managed to obtain partial freedom from serfdom and the far heavier impositions and bondage that weighed upon him in the early days of feudalism, he was still obliged to pay dues and still laboured under the lord's yoke; but within the limits of feudal laws and discretionary powers he enjoyed freedom of movement and relative security of tenure.

Following the normal pattern, trade in agricultural produce developed alongside the social division of labour, and in fact this trade lay largely in the hands of the producers themselves. Thus the key figures in the expanding trade in agricultural produce were the peasants of the small market towns and villages, especially the cattle breeders and cereal- and wine-producers. With the growth of the market the peasantry became a less homogeneous class, and the first signs of capitalist farming thus appeared in the midst of the feudal system, e.g. paid employment of the poorer villagers and of day-labourers, especially on lands owned or rented by wealthy peasants.[1]

But towards the end of the fifteenth century there began in Hungary, as in several other countries in central and eastern Europe, a trend that counteracted both the natural tendency of the peasantry to develop into small-scale bourgeois landowners and the expansion of their market production. This new trend in Hungary may be summed up in economic terms as the growing participation of the nobility in commerce and, subsequently, in the actual production of commercial goods.

There were three successive stages in the process by which the nobles reached this position. First, they exploited their privileged right to sell wine. Second, they took an increasingly active part (especially the big landowners and the lesser nobility) in trade in livestock. Third, they developed their trade in wheat and even their own wheat production.

Let us now consider the first factor in the development of such commercial activity on the part of the nobles: the use they made of their privilege for the sale of wine (*educillatio*). Exercise of this privilege spread increasingly and was bound up with seignorial monopolies. This privilege was not unknown previously, but in the sixteenth century it became a legally recognized source of seignorial revenue throughout the country, and the lords took full advantage of it.

In 1570, a trade decree by the Chamber of Szepes laid down the following: 'passim toto regno [educillatio] receptissima habetur et genus consetur ordinarii proventus.'[2] The law laid down the nobles' exclusive right to sell wine; for those whose estates did not include any vineyards, this right extended from Christmas to Michaelmas (29 September); for those whose estates did include vineyards, from St George's day to Michaelmas, with the right to extend the period.[3] The exercise of this right was generally left to the lord's discretion or to the bailiff of his domain: 'vinorum educillatio fit et exercetur pro arbitrio domini terrestris', as can be found in numerous land registers.[4]

In the exercise of this privilege in selling wines, production by the lord himself was not the dominant financial factor. The lords therefore did their best to increase the quantity of wine available to them for sale. They increased the revenues paid to them in kind, especially those coming from wine-growing peasants. They sought to seize every advantage and to transform vineyard rents that might be paid in cash into rents payable only in kind.[5] For the same reason they tried, in cases where revenues in the form of wine were set at a fixed amount (*jus montium*), to change this fixed amount into a ninth-part tithe (*nona*) on the peasant's entire wine harvest, at any rate when the change was to their advantage.[6] Quite often they also added to their seignorial dues the ecclesiastical tithe on wine (*decima*) which was farmed out to them, and even insisted on their prerogative in the collection of such tithes on their own lands[7] (although they were later forced to recognize the higher claim of the Royal Chamber in districts such as the fortress regions on the borders of the country).[8] Thus they received the tenth (tithe)[9] as well as fixed revenues in kind, or, putting the tenth and the ninth together, they took a *quinta* of the wine produced on peasant vineyards.[10]

Not content with this, the lords also exercised the right of preemption on the wine offered by their serfs for sale—that is, on what was left after deduction of the tenth, the ninth, and sometimes fines also paid in wine.[11] Thus wine sales cannot be said to have taken place on an open market; what we have are, rather, forced sales (at very low prices, perhaps paid for in wheat or not paid for at all), and 'seizure of wine', according to the expression which we find in commercial decrees, land registers and laws passed by the Diet, etc. . . .[12]

Thus increases in wine sales by the nobles meant encroachment upon the peasant wine trade and led to a monopoly of the market. The lord, by taking advantage of provisions stipulating that only his wine could be sold on his domains throughout the greater part of the year, deprived the serf wine-growers of the means of selling their product. The lord further robbed the serfs by requiring payment of revenues in kind, and by demanding wine in payment of other dues, and thus took from them a large portion of their market yield; it all amounted to a constantly increasing seizure of peasant produce. As a result, wine consumers in the villages might find themselves buying at high prices in the lord's wine shops the very wine which their lord had got from them at no cost, in the form of revenues paid in kind, or bought from them at a minimal price or even taken from them by force. This first form of trade on the part of the lords severely reduced peasant market production in one of the most important branches of agriculture.

The second phase in the development of the nobles' commercial activity consisted in active participation by the large landowners and the middle nobility in the livestock trade. This activity, which for the nobles was a new one, had started early in the sixteenth century,[13] but did not become important until after the battle of Mohács (1526). In contrast to the village wine and livestock trade, where sales outside the area and exports (for instance to Moravia or Poland)[14] played only a minor role (though a sizeable one even so), the nobility's participation in the livestock trade in the sixteenth century grew chiefly through exports—to Vienna, the towns of the German Empire (Augsburg, Nuremburg), Moravia, Venice and other towns of northern Italy. This large-scale export trade on the part of the nobles, involving some tens of thousands of animals sold to western countries, represented the major part of Hungary's total annual exports. These first two phases in the development of the nobles' trade—in livestock and in wine—depended only to a very small extent on the produce of their own lands. The majority of the herds of oxen taken to the markets came from peasant farms. But with oxen there was the difference that the lords of the western region of the country, which was under Hapsburg rule, did not trade in animals obtained from their serfs (as they did with wine) but were generally content to take an active part in the extensive cattle trade stemming from the large *puszta* around the towns of the great Hungarian plain in the lands that had fallen to the Turks. Livestock changed hands on the great markets of the western provinces and elsewhere. Exporters then sent the herds on to Austria and Moravia.[15]

In these western regions of Hungary under Hapsburg domination the great lords were, in ever-growing numbers, engaging in wholesale and export trade in livestock with the help of agents (*factores mercenarii*), and this activity developed alongside and at the expense of that of the stock-raisers of the Great Plain and the large-scale traders, who had risen principally from the ranks of the prosperous peasants and bourgeoisie. In the 1520s, György of Brandenburg, the owner of the domain of Gyula, several times bought cattle from the peasant breeders of the village of Gyula for export to Silesia. Pál Bakits, a great landowner in the county of Pozsony, passed the customs barrier at Esztergom in 1535 with 2,000 oxen. According to the registers recording payment of the *traite* (thirtieth), established in 1542, about 12 per cent of the export trade in oxen was conducted by the following lords: Renenc Nyáry, Imre Balassa, Sebestyén Thököly, Ferenc Révay, Anna Pekry. About the middle of the century István Dobó, Ferenc Say and Sebestyén Bornemissza, all bearers of illustrious names, went into partnership to trade in oxen, selling them in Hungary and exporting them to Vienna. In 1544 Gáspár Serédi and in 1563 Menyhért Balassa obtained licences for the duty-free export of 1,000 oxen each; in 1580 Gábor Kendi, Péter Krusith and his heirs, Gyula Salm and others obtained export licences for large consignments exempt from the *traite*. The Palatine, Támas Nádasdy and the supreme captain of Gyula, László Kerechényi, often bought up beef stock to resell it at a profit or export it to Austria. About the end of the century, the Zrinyi were delivering oxen to Venice. But the great lords were not alone in this trade; large numbers of the middle and lesser nobility also took part.[16]

Naturally the lords and nobles used their privileges to gain every advantage over their peasant and bourgeois competitors. They not only obtained regular renewal of their exemptions from inland duty,[17] in particular on 'oxen being transported from one place to another within the country',[18] but also gained exemption from customs charges on exports, at least 'for animals reared on their own seignorial farms'.[19] They then took steps to include in this category oxen that they had bought for export without payment of the *traite*.[20] Although the law expressly charged dues (*traite*) on goods purchased for commerce and subsequently exported,[21] and furthermore laid down that export of *propri allodiatura* (produce from the demesne) required a licence,[22] these obstacles were freely circumvented: 'Die hungarischen Herrn ... schreiben Mautbrief, dass mann frei passieren soll lassen', reported the captain in charge of the mining region as early as the middle of the century.[23]

As participation by lords and nobles in the livestock trade increased, so the activity of peasant and bourgeois traders was considerably reduced. It is no surprise, therefore, to learn that in 1574 'the citizens of the free and mining towns' presented a petition to the Diet asking that 'lords and nobles should not be allowed to trade in leather, horses, livestock and similar goods'. There is hardly any need to add that the Estates, far from approving this petition, decided that 'the great lords, and the nobles as well, might freely engage in trade in any types of goods'.[24] Thus peasant trade was progressively eliminated in this field too.

The third stage in the development of trade on the part of the lords was wheat marketing. In 1542 a certain great Hungarian lord wrote: 'Est mihi animus, ut emam unam navem, quae mille metretas ordei et tritici ferre potest. Ordeum, farinam et alia victualia mecum ducam.'[25] Such ideas were put into practice. As early as the middle of the sixteenth century a large number of seignorial domains were producing wheat for the market: among them the estates of Nádasdy, Dobó, Forgách, Drugeth, Perényi, Choron and others. Revenue for the estates of the fortress of Gyula from the sale of wheat rose from 225 florins in 1519, to 627 in 1527 and 2,808 in 1557.

Export of wheat did not take place on a very large scale;[26] nor did enforced sales to villagers constitute an important factor, although certain instances are related of the lord using undisguised force to sell the wheat from his domains—and spoiled wheat at that—to his own serfs.[27] Such compulsory sales were less extensively made in respect of wheat than wine. We must point out in this connection a related problem, which, it is true, is of a different kind, but still of great interest: it concerns the heavy demand for agricultural produce on the part of impoverished peasants and manual workers without tenure; the degree to which the well-to-do peasants profited by unloading surplus produce on this extensive sector of the home market, and the part played by seignorial produce in the same market.[28] The question requires more research but in any case there is evidence that impoverished serfs bought wheat and other produce from their own lords.[29]

In the wheat sector as in the two others, research done shows that seignorial trade could make progress in town markets only at the expense of peasant producers. We may note for instance that in the 1570s the wheat suppliers to the town of Selmecbánya were István Dobó, Imre Forgách, Gábor Dóczy and Zsigmond Pándi, all four great feudal landowners.[30] In this, as in the two other sectors, the nobles made full use of their privileges to gain commercial advantage. Nothing could be easier for them than to evade payment of duties on wheat grown for the most part on their own demesnes and brought into towns near their estates. They took over the supply of wheat and fodder to the armies, in particular the armies of mercenaries billeted on the country, and the frontier fortresses. Through their sales to the national exchequer during the favourable market conditions in the wars with the Turks, which had become more or less permanent, an important new commercial outlet was opened for them, and if we bear in mind the rise in prices throughout Europe we can easily understand how great landowners, especially those with influential connections, made vast profits as they rose to high positions in politics or the army.[31]

In fact the wheat which the nobles brought on to the market came from the same source as the wine they sold: a rising proportion of the peasants' harvest was taken by the nobles for this purpose, either in the form of revenues paid in kind ('ninths' of the wheat yield and other revenues), or by means of bulk purchase. In order to increase revenues payable by serfs in the form of wheat, the great landowners adopted a wide variety of methods. Sometimes they would raise the rate of fixed annual revenues (*aconalia*), sometimes they would replace them by the *nona* (ninths)—which was the most widespread method—or, when the peasant had previously bought the right to pay the ninth in cash, the lord forced him once more to pay in kind (*in specie*).[32] Payment in ninths became even more widespread in respect to the wheat yield than for wine;[33] it was often joined to the tenth and the two together made up the tax, farmed out by the church, known as the *quinta*.[34] Another means of increasing revenues paid in wheat, although less widespread, achieved the same result: the serfs were deprived of their tenure and compensated with small strips of land of a few acres, paid for by rent consisting of a quarter or a fifth of the harvest.[35] Apart from these measures, although the lords did not enjoy the right of pre-emption, as they did for wine, they still often 'bought' or 'borrowed' wheat from their peasants by force, paying much less than the current price; and it is clear that their purpose was to resell at a profit.[36]

The measures described above had the same effects as in the wine and cattle trades. The peasants' share of the market contracted, and eventually production on their land was permanently reduced. The nobles' requirements in wheat marketing affected the whole structure of feudal revenues: rent paid in kind took on a new importance in relation to cash rents. On an estate such as that of the Archbishopric of Esztergom, for instance, where at the close of the previous century rent in cash had been preferred to rent in kind,[37] we note that in the years 1568–70 and 1581–4 income from revenues paid in the form of wheat (i.e. the ninth and the tenth) equalled income from revenues previously paid in cash—which included income from farming the demesne.[38] In 1575 in the Tokaj district the value of revenues in kind was several times greater than the cash payments received;[39] and we could cite other examples. . . . From this trend, i.e. the return to payment in kind, we can conclude that payments in the form of wheat and wine, taken as a proportion of the harvest, had gradually become the main forms of feudal dues paid by the serfs of Hungary.[40]

But the nobles' growing participation in the wheat trade was a severer blow to market production by the peasants than the expansion of the nobles' trade in wine and livestock, for it was as a result of this activity that the lords turned their attention more and more to the cultivation of their own lands, to the cost of their serfs. This third type of commercial activity, wheat marketing, proved to be one of the chief stimuli to the expansion of the demesnes and of direct farming undertaken with the aim of increasing yields. In contrast to developments in the wine and cattle trade, sales of wheat produced on the demesnes were in several regions soon able to gain ground not only over the produce of peasant tenures, but also over that of the rapidly growing *terra indominicata*. The estate of Gyula is a highly characteristic example of this: in 1519 wheat sales brought in 225 florins and this figure represented only sales of wheat levied as payment of the ninth; in 1557 income was over twelve times as great, and this considerable sum was essentially the result of farming of the demesne.[41]

The excellent opportunities offered by trade and commerce, and the increased food requirements of the courts of the great lords and the rich, also stimulated the development of farming on the demesnes whether they were in private or royal possession. Food for private armies and the king's mercenary troops had to be supplied directly, without actual purchase, and the same held for supplies to the courts of the nobles, and for the lords' domestic requirements, which were constantly on the increase. This factor in the development of farming, which was no less important, is brought out by an instruction from Munkács, issued in 1570, according to which farming of the demesne 'was to take precedence over all else' and was necessary for the following reasons: 'ex ea potissimum loci sustentatio pendeat et alimenta praesidii reponi soleant.'[42] Direct supplies to the court, the troops and the border fortresses meant that in many cases the major part of the produce paid by serfs in dues or harvested on the seignorial demesnes was allocated automatically.[43] We must stress that besides actual commerce on the part of the nobles, consumption on the seignorial estates also impeded market production by the peasantry. When we find in the detailed accounts for the Nádasdy estates almost only special commodities (spices, citrus fruits), 'wine and victuals always being at hand',[44] and since the instruction from Munkács mentioned above provided for the rearing of cows and poultry and the growing of fruit on estates in order to ensure supplies of dairy produce, eggs, vegetables and so on 'without need to purchase', or to 'avoid superfluous expenditure',[45] we must recognize this to be evidence of efforts to stifle the peasant market, which had previously enjoyed a measure of prosperity as a result of demand on the part of the estates at the time when they received revenues only in cash.

From the 1530s and 1540s onwards the *allodia*—a Latin term used generally in Hungary to designate farmed demesnes—had appeared in considerable numbers, especially in the western regions under Hapsburg rule: the part of Transdanubia not occupied by the Turks, the western and central regions of north Hungary (Slovakia), and especially the domains of the great lords and the royal estates and even the estates of the lesser nobility. By the middle of the century there were few regions in the 'royal' Hungary of the Hapsburgs without seignorial demesnes. About the middle of the century a great landowner such as Támas Nádasdy possessed more than a dozen farms which were exploited directly, quite apart from his own estate at Sárvár Kapuvár;[46] there was also his property at Léka where, in 1549 and in 1557, two new demesnes were created;[47] and also his property at Kanizsa where, in 1564, despite the constant threat of Turkish attack, seven direct farming enterprises continued to operate.[48] From 1532 onwards the county of Pozsony (Bratislava) saw the appearance of demesnes[49] on the properties of Gáspár Serédi, Pál Bakits and Elek Thurzó; and in the county of Szepes the land register, drawn up in 1564–5 on the estates of the Thurzó family, refers to two of these: 'the old' and 'the new'. In 1570 the land register of the Szendrö district mentioned wheat-fields farmed directly[50] in fourteen villages, and that of Sárospatak mentioned the same in seven villages.

In contrast with the earlier practice of keeping relatively small areas of land for seignorial farming,[51] expansion of the system of direct management began with the cultivation of the fallow land of the villages and of land not being used for agricultural purposes; it then progressed by means of forest clearance and reclamation of pasture and grazing land. This sort of expansion thus went on at the expense of the serfs, depriving them of their rights to common use of the forest and their common grazing rights. Land-holdings left by serfs were taken over,[52] and even tillage forming part of inhabited holdings was incorporated into the demesnes or otherwise annexed to the seignorial reserve. In some cases we meet direct seizure of the land or total or partial expropriation of peasant tenures.[53] The land register for the Csejte domain, dating from 1568, mentions serfs 'quorum terrae coluntur domino terrestri', and who for this reason were excused payment of rent. The document dealing with direct farming of the cameral domain of Szatmár, drawn up in 1572 for the Chamber of Szepes, states that all the demesnes had been created on land taken from the serfs 'cum injuria eorum'.[54] On the domain of Kapuvár, in the 1580s, the serf lived as a labourer without land (*inquilinus*), his holding being worked by the lord's plough and treated as belonging to the demesne.[55] It is indicative of this situation that from the middle of the century onwards the law made a distinction between 'land belonging directly to the nearby estate' and that which 'was taken from the serfs and recently appropriated for the purpose of farming as part of the demesne'.[56]

The demesnes (for the most part arable land, grazing land, vineyards, fish ponds), the area of which continued to increase as a result of the methods we have already mentioned, were farmed partly by means of the corvee (*servitium, labor*) performed by the serfs who worked with their own tools and their own beasts of burden. Thus, this method of direct farming yielded an income additional to produce revenues, and led in the end to the extension of the other natural form of feudal revenue, rent paid in labour. Whereas in the years 1510–20, one day of compulsory labour was the rule, according to the laws of 1514[57] (at least on the large seignorial properties), and this in fact was often not enforced,[58] by the middle of the century the situation was very different. This change finds expression in the provisions of the law of 1548, defining the corvee to be carried out on demesnes for the five following types of work: ploughing, sowing, haymaking, harvesting, wine-growing, to which must be added haulage of wine and other produce—and already authorizing the lord to demand two days of corvee in the wine-growing, hay harvest and harvest seasons.[59] The ever-mounting burden of the corvee is also described in a number of sources. The land register for the domain of Gyula (1525) required only two days of labour for scything and one day at harvest-time; but in the same book, entries for 1559 and 1561 tell of serfs being generally required 'to carry out all the work and services', 'to plough, sow and attend to other tasks as well'.[60] Whereas in 1530 the land register for the domain of Kanizsa mentions a relatively slight corvee, letters written by serfs in the 1550s complain of the unbearable increase in the corvee, quite apart from the frequent illegal seizures of land.[61] The workers on the estate of Pozsony, previously required to work seven days of corvee per year, were in 1574 forced to work a total corvee of 60 days.[62] At Krasznahorka in 1578 the lord 'cogit eos toties, quoties opus est'.[63] In 1570 the villages belonging to the domain of Szendrö unanimously complained of 'intolerable servitude'; they were so burdened by the corvee that they had no time left for cultivation of their own vineyards and fields; the same is true of the domain of Tokaj where, according to the 1581 land register, the serfs were often required to carry out domanial corvee without any free days for two or three weeks on end.

In another respect, the development of commerce based on the farming of demesnes went hand-in-hand with the utilization, on a fairly large scale, of domanial equipment and paid labour, where servants, farm lads, gardeners, shepherds, harvesters and day-labourers were partly recruited from the impoverished and expropriated peasantry.

There had already been some mention of servants and farm lads ('mercenarii et alii servitores nobilium, qui proprio victu et amictu dominorum suorum utuntur') in the laws and estate documents dating from before the Mohács disaster.[64] In the following decades we come across them frequently in accounts, land registers and instructions under various titles—*allodiator, allodiatrix, mercenarii et servitores allodiorum, pastores in allodiis, hortulanus*, etc. . . .[65] They are mostly mentioned together with certain pieces of equipment on the demesne, for instance 'farm hands with plough'.[66] Some other examples: in 1572 the steward of the cameral estate of Szatmár proposed that the Chamber of Szepes should, for the four farms being directly farmed, in addition to a higher rate of corvee, provide four ploughs with eight oxen and three farm servants, who were probably not all adults, for we read 'there are some men with two or three children in their care who can be taken on'.[67] The landowners also called upon seasonal workers in addition to their regular hands ('diverses laboratores tam vinearum dominii, quam agriculturas allodiorum'),[68] day-labourers for the harvest and for reaping, harvesters and reapers paid in kind, hoers and vine-workers, etc. . . .[69]

This practice is explained by the fact that previous trends could not immediately be reversed; the corvee which had, in the previous century, played a very limited role, could not suddenly be greatly increased to the new requirements of direct farming, and, at least for a time, the lords were forced to employ some paid labour.[70]

This phenomenon can be seen in certain mixed forms of working relationships: the same serfs carried out certain forms of work sometimes free and sometimes for payment; they were sometimes paid (in cash or in kind) for the work done as corvee, sometimes paid only for that part of the work done in addition to the corvee; sometimes the lord's oxen were used in the corvee; sometimes a serf with tenure was made to work as a farm-hand, and so on. The land register of Gyula, drawn up in 1525, laid down that workers from the town were to thresh the wheat from the demesne in fulfilment of the corvee due from them, but guaranteed them a tenth part of the threshed wheat. The land register for Világosvár in the same year laid down special dues to be paid in money to cover the cost of wages paid to the farm lads who had been recruited by the captain from among the 'good serfs', that is those with tenure. According to the land registers of Esztergom, drawn up in 1527 and 1553, all reaping, hay-harvesting and harvesting required of serfs in the form of corvee were to be paid in wages.[71] When in 1554 the land register of Hédervár laid down that rent was to be paid in labour instead of in money, and was to become due on St George's day and at Michaelmas, it stated that any agricultural work which could not be carried out as corvee was to be carried out by the serfs 'for money paid by the lord'. The land register of Eger, drawn up in 1558, laid down the general obligation that work should be carried out free, but it nevertheless provided for any work carried out in addition to the corvee (reaping, for example) to be paid in wages (allowed on rent due at Michaelmas), and finally, in exchange for certain forms of work (for instance, work carried out within the fortress), it provided for payment of a daily wage, in cash or in the form of goods. In 1562, the serfs of Komárom received a cube of salt per day for their corvee, done in the form of reaping; reapers carrying out the corvee in the domain of Nagybánya received foodstuffs as payment for their work in 1566 and for work carried out in addition to the corvee they received wages (although this was still a sum well below the wages of a day-worker). The land register of Szendrö, drawn up in 1570, tells us that about the middle of the century farm-hands received wages paid in money and that the sum used to meet these costs represented dues paid in cash by the serfs. According to the land register of Pozsony (1574), certain villages were required to provide reapers for the demesne as well as harvesters to whom daily wages were paid (although such wages were below the usual rate); labourers who had previously benefited from a food allowance granted during the period of the corvee continued to do so but received wages in the form of money for work done in the vineyards. If we may accept the evidence of the land register of the domain of Tokaj, drawn up in 1581, only a certain number of the vineyards of the demesne were cultivated by means of the corvee; on the rest, work was carried out in return for cash wages. In some cases, the steward had substituted work in the vineyards for payment of rent at Martinmas.[72] Paid work was combined with the corvee but it was none the less always in the grip of the feudal system and exacted under duress.

Thus the new trends in Hungarian agriculture in the sixteenth century are extension of the demesne at the expense of peasant holdings, extension of seignorial commercial production and an increase in the use of paid forms of labour.

The development of trade and market production on the part of the Hungarian nobles in the sixteenth century differs sharply from what happened in the countries of western Europe (France in particular).[73] However, this divergence of Hungarian development will not seem unique in all respects if it is compared with English developments in the same period, which followed a similar path. We refer to the 'new nobility', the English 'gentry', which received rent due as feudal revenue largely in the form of cash. This class engaged in trade in wool, wheat and other goods, and after expropriating the peasants and small-scale farmers, undertook direct farming of its own lands, as was typical of capitalist economy, and progressively took on bourgeois character-istics.[74]

The Hungarian lords of the sixteenth century, as we read in a document from the year 1550, 'devoted themselves to trade, engaging merchants and dealers in livestock, cloth, lead, copper and all manner of things';[75] as we learn from another source for that period, they 'built up large stocks of wine, wheat, meat and other foodstuffs, waiting for prices to rise in order to sell them at four times their value';[76] as we have seen, they enlarged their demesnes by seizing peasant holdings if need be, and making use of paid labour on their domains. Thus these Hungarian lords of the sixteenth century, from many points of view, showed bourgeois characteristics similar to those of the English gentry.

However, there was still a marked feudal aspect to the Hungarian trader-cum-farmer lord of the sixteenth century. As a trader, he took advantage of his feudal prerogatives and the pressure he could apply outside the economic sphere; in order to ensure commercial success he created a forced market (let us simply mention in this connection the sale of seignorial wine to local customers and the seizure of the wine trade in villages); he employed his privileges as a nobleman (in the wheat and livestock trade) against his peasant and bourgeois competitors, and, by means of the 'ninth' on wheat and wine and other dues paid in kind, derived ever-increasing profit from feudal rent. As a producer he made a rising profit from that other form of feudal income, the forced labour of his serfs. This second characteristic of the Hungarian lord distinguishes him from his English counterpart and brings out the essential nature of the conditions prevailing in central and eastern regions of Europe (German territories east of the Elbe, Bohemia,

Poland) where the type of agriculture known as *Gutsherr* farming developed.[77]

These features become increasingly important during the last decades of the sixteenth century. In the first half of the seventeenth, *Gutswirtschaft*, based on the corvee, became the main system of farming, and the divorce between Hungarian agricultural development and that of western Europe was complete.[78]

Notes

1 For more detailed information, see Z. P. Pach, 'Das Entwicklungsniveau der feudalen Agrarverhältnisse in Ungarn in der zweiten Hälfte des XV. Jahrhunderts', *Studia Historica Acad. Sci. Hung.*, vol. 46, Budapest, 1960.

2 *Magyar Gazdaságtörténeti Szemle (M.Gt.Sz.) (Hungarian Economic History Review)*, 1896, p. 70. The land registers of the Kapuvár district, about the end of the 15th and the beginning of the 16th century; *Országos Levéltár* (OL) (*National Archives*), *Collection of Documents before 1526* (Dl.): 36 992; 36 983; 37 007 do not mention this; however the selling of seignorial wine is mentioned in the document for 1584 as an 'old custom'. (OL) '*Urbaria et Conscriptiones*' (*U. et C.*) 56:33.

3 Article 36 of the law of 1550. Cf. OL, *U. et C.*, 26:67.

4 For example, Szendrö: 1570; Tokaj: 1581. See: *Urbáriumok XVI–XVII század* (16th- and 17th- Century Land Registers), ed. E. Maksay, Budapest, 1959. All land registers which are referred to without reference number are to be found in this work.

5 See for example the complaint made by the serfs of Iharos to their lord in 1551: 'It used to be customary on our vineyard for us to pay our tithe in money; but after the last two wine harvests it was taken in the form of wine.' *Magyar Müvelödéstörténet* (*History of Hungarian Civilization*), vol. III, Budapest (no date), pp. 116–17. A similar complaint was made in the same year by the inhabitants of the market town of Somogycsicsó against the taking of the wine tithe in kind instead of cash: *Jobbágylevelek* (*Serfs' Letters*), ed. E. H. Balazs, Budapest, 1951, pp. 21–2. The land register for the Vöröskö district for 1543 records that money-rents paid for vineyards and fixed-amount payments in kind were changed into ninth-part tithes. *Urbáre feudálnych panstiev na Slovensku. XVI storocie*, R. Marsina and M. Kusik, vol. I, Bratislava, 1959, pp. 69 et seq.

6 Regarding the ninth-part wine tithe, cf. for example the land registers of the Léva district, 1554 (OL, *U. et C.*, 16:5); the Palota district, 1578; the

estates of the nuns of Somlóvásárhely, 1593 (transcribed text), *Történelmi Tár* (*T.T.*) (*Historical Journal*), 1903, pp. 414–19.

7 Article 35 of the law of 1547; article 61 of the law of 1548; article 43 of the law of 1556.

8 Article 68 of the law of 1563; article 27 of the law of 1569; article 22 of the law of 1574.

9 See, for example, the decree for the Kanizsa and Sztenyicsnyák districts of 1564, *M. Gt. Sz.*, 1896, pp. 67–8, 72–3.

10 See, for example, the land registers of the Csábrág and Eger districts, 1558; the Vác district, 1578; Tokaj, 1581; or the tithes (tenths and ninths) taken on wine in 1561 by the fortress of Gyula. The latter in *Gyula város okleveltára* (*Archives of the Town of Gyula*), Budapest, 1938, p. 353. Other examples of the compounding of the ninth and the tenth taken on wine by nobles at the beginning of the 16th century: OL, Dl. 37 007, 104 125.

11 Article 36 of the law of 1550.

12 Cf., for example, the decree of the Munkács district of 1570: *M. Gt. Sz.*, 1896, p. 70; land register for Szendrö of the same year; article 21 of the law of 1574.

13 It will be rightly assumed that the restrictive laws on livestock trade, issued by the Diets of the time, reflected the efforts of the nobles who engaged in livestock trade and tried to get rid of their competitors (Cf. I. Szabó, 'A hajduk 1514-ben' ('The Hajduks in 1514'), *Szazadok* (*Centuries*), 1950, pp. 194–6). Thus the lesser nobility said of Ambrus Sárkány, Grand Judge, in 1525: 'You were trading in wine and livestock, you were oppressing the poor, while we protected the frontiers'; V. Fraknói, *Magyarország a mohácsi vész elött a pápai követek jelentései alapján* (*Hungary before the Disaster of Mohács in the Light of Reports by Papal Nuncios*), Budapest, 1884, p. 147.

14 *M. Gt. Sz.*, 1894, pp. 108–9, etc. Cf. article 38 of the law of 1567; article 35 of the law of 1595.

15 For the chief features of the livestock trade see: S. Takats, *Rajzok a török világból* (*Sketches from the Time of the Turkish Occupation*), vol. III, Budapest, 1917, pp. 8 et seq.; for its extent: Gy. Ember, 'Külkereskedelmünk történetéhez a XVI. században' ('Data on the History of our Foreign Trade in the 16th Century'), published in *A Magyar Tudományos Akadémia Társadalmi-Történeti Tudományok Osztályának Közleményei*, vol. 8, no. 4, Budapest, 1958, pp. 335–8. According to this work, in 1542—if we are to accept the evidence of accounts registers for the 'thirtieth' (customs dues)— with the exception of copper and precious metals, which represented $\frac{4}{5}$ of the total volume, 93·4% of the total volume of Hungarian exports to the west consisted of cattle, mainly oxen. In 1542, 27,529 oxen were exported to Austria and Moravia. The total volume of cattle exports appears to have increased subsequently. In the period 1549–51 the Hungarian traders sold

more than 180,000 oxen on the markets held weekly in Vienna: S. Takats, *Szégeny magyarok (Poor Hungarians)*, Budapest (no date), p. 135. In 1588 more than 84,000 oxen passed over the bridge of Ersekujvár (*M. Gt. Sz.*, 1897, p. 194). Cf. *Budai török számadáskönyvek (Turkish Accounts Registers)*, *1550–1580*, published by L. Fekete and Gy. Kaldy-Nagy, Budapest, 1962, p. 588 et seq.

16 *Archives of the Town of Gyula*, pp. 77–9, 84, 101–2, 126, 152; J. Hornyik, *Kecskemét város története (History of the Town of Kecskemét)*, vol. I, Kecskemét, 1860, p. 235; *M. Gt. Sz.*, 1898, p. 422, and 1899, pp. 250–1; I. Acsady, *Közgazdasági állopotaink a XVI. és XVII. században (Economic Situation of Hungary in the 16th and 17th Centuries)*, Budapest, 1899, pp. 62–3; S. Takats, op.cit. *(Poor Hungarians)*, pp. 143–4; Gy. Komoróczy, *Nádasdy Tamás és a XVI. századi magyar nagybirtok gazdálkodása (Tamás Nádasdy and Large-scale Estate Management in the 16th Century in Hungary)*, Budapest, 1932, p. 106; Gy. Ember, *Magyarország XVI. századi külkereskedelmének történetéhez (Contributions to the History of the Export Trade of Hungary in the 16th Century)*, Századok, 1961, no. 1, p. 40, etc.

17 Article 26 of the law of 1543; article 55 of the law of 1548, etc.

18 Article 18 of the law of 1553; article 16 of the law of 1557.

19 Article 36 of the law of 1567; article 17 of the law of 1569; article 25 of the law of 1574, etc.

20 The frauds committed by the lords and nobles engaged in this commerce in evading the *traite* were described in detail in article 44 of the law of 1559— among such frauds was that of marketing large numbers of animals that had been purchased but which were presented as stock reared on the seignorial reserve. Cf. *M. Gt. Sz.*, 1896, p. 73.

21 Article 37 of the law of 1574.

22 Article 34 of the law of 1599.

23 Takats, op.cit. *(Poor Hungarians)*, p. 143.

24 Article 24 of the law of 1574.

25 *Archives of the Hédervány Family (Héderváry oklt.)*, vol. II, Budapest, 1922, p. 122.

26 Komoróczy, op.cit., pp. 102–6; J. Belitzky, *A magyar gabonakivitel története (History of Wheat Exporting in Hungary)*, Budapest, 1932, p. 27; *Archives of the Town of Gyula*, pp. 74, 99, 383.

27 For exportation of wheat to Austria, see *M. Gt. Sz.*, 1900, pp. 242, 252; for exportation to Venice, *M. Gt. Sz.*, 1899, pp. 241–2. At all events wheat exports from Hungary were still not very great in the 16th century. Wine exports were far more extensive (especially to the north) but were far from being as extensive as livestock exports, which were considerable.

28 Cf. *M. Gt. Sz.*, 1896, p. 70; *Archives of the Town of Gyula*, pp. 301, 387. Cf. I. Szabo, *Tanulmányok a magyar parasztság történetéböl (Studies in the History of the Hungarian Peasantry)*, Budapest, 1948, p. 188.

29 *Archives of the Town of Gyula*, p. 299; L. Ruzsas, *Az egri vár gazdálkodása a*
    XVI. században (*Management of the Fortress of Eger in the 16th Century*),
    Budapest, 1939, pp. 35, 39.

30 J. Sobó, *Selmecbánya sz. kir. város társadalma, ipara és kereskedelme a XVI.*
    század második felében (*Society, Industry and Commerce in the Royal Free Town*
    of Selmecbánya in the Second Half of the 16th Century), Budapest, 1910,
    pp. 31–6.

31 Concerning the business transactions of one of the greatest military
    suppliers, who was a noble, see P. Jedlicska, *Adatok erdödi báró Pálffy Miklós,*
    a györi hösnek életrajza—és korához 1552–1590 (*Facts concerning the Life and*
    Times of Miklós Pálffy, Baron of Erdöd, the Hero of Györ), Eger, 1897, pp. 116,
    184, 298, 614, etc. The importance of the economic factors resulting from
    the wars and the armies' requirements in foodstuffs has already been brought
    out in previous research, but the view taken of the relationship between the
    political and economic role of the great lords of the 16th century is open to
    criticism. G. F. Knapp's theory (*Die Bauernbefreiung und der Ursprung der*
    Landarbeiter in den älteren Teilen Preussens, vol. I, 2nd ed., Munich-Leipzig,
    1927, p. 37), emphasizing the progressive decline of the military role played
    by the great landowning knights and attributing the development of the
    lords' economic role to their exclusion from 'national affairs' and public
    life by the central authority, has been supported by some historians; cf.
    I. Wellmann, 'Mezörógazdaságtörténetünk uj utja' ('New views on the
    history of Hungarian agriculture'), in *Domanovszky emlékkönyv*, Budapest,
    1937, pp. 684–6. But this conception has proved to be untenable.

32 For increase in fixed revenues, see Léka and Sárvár (OL, Dl., 37 007
    (1519)); for replacement of fixed revenues by the ninth, see the Komárom
    domain (OL, U. et C., 4:45 (1592)); for suppression of the right to
    buy back for cash, cf. land register for Pilis Abbey (OL, U. et C., 62:32
    (1578)).

33 See, for example, the land registers of the domain of Kanizsa (1530), Gyula
    (1560), of the provost's domain of Lelesz (1566) (OL, U. et C., 18:15), the
    domain of Sztropko (1569), and *Urbáre feudálnych panstiev na Slovensku*,
    vol. I, pp. 239–40.

34 See respectively Murány (1573), Csábrág (1558), Munkács (1570) (*M.*
    Gt. Sz., 1896, p. 69), Krasznahorka (1570) (OL, U. et C., 2:22).

35 *Magyar Országgyulési Emlékek* (*Documents from the Hungarian Diets*), vol. V,
    Budapest, 1877, p. 432 (1572).

36 Article 44 of the law of 1559: *Magyar Országgyulési Emlékek*, vol. IV,
    Budapest, 1877, p. 563 (1563); *M. Gt. Sz.*, 1900, p. 252 (1570).

37 F. Fügedi, *Az esztergomi érsekség gazdálkodása a XV. század végén* (*Finances of*
    the Archbishopric of Esztergom at the close of the 15th Century), Századok, 1960,
    nos. 1–3, pp. 90 et seq.

38 *M. Gt. Sz.*, 1905, p. 175, and 1894, pp. 35–6. See *Urbáre feudálnych*

panstiev na Slovensku, vol. I, pp. 278 et seq., also OL, *U. et C.*, 45:28 (1571 and 1597).

39 As has been shown by I. Acsady, *M. Gt. Sz.*, 1895, p. 135. See I. N. Kiss, 'Uradalmi gazdálkodás Sárospatakon és Tokajban a XVI. század második felében' ('Seignorial management at Sárospatak and Tokaj in the Second Half of the 16th Century'), in *Történelmi Szemle (Historical Journal)*, 1960, no. 1, pp. 22–4.

40 See Z. P. Pach, 'Neuvième et dixième prélevés par les seigneurs au XVIIᵉ siècle', in *Nouvelles Études historiques publiés par la Commission Nationale des Historiens Hongrois*, Budapest, 1965, pp. 417 et seq.

41 *Archives of the Town of Gyula*, pp. 74, 383.

42 *M. Gt. Sz.*, 1896, pp. 67, 70.

43 See, for example, J. Holub, *Egy dunántuli egyházi nagybirtok élete a középkor végén (A Large Ecclesiastical Estate in Transdanubia at the End of the Middle Ages)*, Pécs, 1943, pp. 39–40; F. Maksay, *Parasztság és majorgazdálkodás a XVI. századi Magyarországon (The Peasantry and Demesne Farming on the Part of the Nobles in Hungary in the 16th Century)*, Budapest, 1948, pp. 18–19, 22.

44 Komoróczy, op.cit., p. 109.

45 *M. Gt. Sz.*, 1896, pp. 68, 75. Cf. '. . . to ensure that the desmesne is farmed and beasts reared there, so that we are not forced to pay cash the whole time, but in a position to sell and derive profit from so doing. . .' (*Archives of the Town of Gyula*, pp. 77–9).

46 Komoróczy, op.cit., p. 62; J. Tholt, *A sárvári uradalom majorgazdálkodasa a XVII. századd elsö felében (Farming of the Demesne at Sárvár in the First Half of the 17th Century)*, Budapest, 1934, pp. 13–18.

47 *Levéltári Közlemények (Archives Bulletin)*, 1929, p. 234; *T.T.*, 1911, pp. 448–9.

48 *M. Gt. Sz.*, 1894, p. 71.

49 Maksay, op.cit., pp. 25–9.

50 The land registers for Szepesvár and Szendrö for 1570 were recently published in the work quoted above; the land register for the Sárospatak estate for the same year: OL, *U. et C.*, 95:22.

51 K. Taganyi, *A földközösseg története Magyarországon (The History of Community Ownership of Land in Hungary)*, 2nd ed., Budapest (no date), pp. 58–9.

52 See the land registers for Nagytapolcsány (1570) (OL, *U. et C.*, 60:70) and Szepesvár (1596) (OL, *U. et C.*, 49:17). This does not mean that seizure of abandoned peasant holdings was general practice.

53 The case, which is in fact fairly frequent, of the lord joining to his estate a holding 'freely' given up by an impoverished serf forms a transition between the two methods of seizure: annexation of a vacant holding and occupation of an inhabited holding.

54 OL, *Városi és Kamarai Iratok (Municipal and Cameral Documents)*, Fol. lat. 913. Cf. 'Agoston, the Provost, arranged for a large arable field to be occupied by force.' OL, *U. et C.*, 8:15 (1566): 'Ferenc Bebek occupied the best land, which had formerly been part of peasant holdings, in order to join it to his nearby estate, leaving them [i.e. the serfs of Krasznahorkaváral ja] tenures only of inferior quality.' OL, *U. et C.*, 2:22 (1570); the same document gives information on the seizure of vineyards and grazing land

55 OL, *U. et C.*, 56:33 (1584). The same land register relates the following facts concerning one of the villages (Pordány): 'Before the conquest of Buda (1541), the serfs possessed a whole holding there. But after direct seignorial farming had been introduced there and fields and pastures used for this purpose, the serfs were reduced to possession of half a holding.'

56 Article 70 of the law of 1563.

57 These laws formed part of the repressive measures taken as a result of the peasants' revolt of 1514. Services rendered by serfs, including the corvee, which was established at one day per week, were controlled by articles 15–20 of the law of 1514.

58 See, for example, Léka: 1519 (OL, Dl., 37 007); Kisvárda: 1521, *A zichi és vasönkeöi gróf Zichy-család idösb ágának okmánytára (Archives of the Line of the Eldest Sons of the Zichy Family, from Zichy and Vasonkeo)*, vol. XII, Budapest, 1931, pp. 343–64; Világosvár: 1525 (OL, Dl., 37 000).

59 Articles 33–8 of the law of 1548; cf. articles 10–12 of the law of 1553.

60 *Archives of the Town of Gyula*, pp. 88, 289, 348.

61 OL, *U. et C.*, 27:55; *Serf Letters*, pp. 25–31.

62 OL, *U. et C.*, 34:74.

63 OL, *U. et C.*, 82–9. See Tapolca (1570), OL, *U. et C.*, 61:71; Léva (1589), OL, *U. et C.*, 16:5; Szepesvár (1596), OL, *U. et C.*, 49:17.

64 Article 1 of the law of 1522; article 24 of the law of 1523; *Archives of the Town of Gyula*, p. 86; OL, Dl., 37 000.

65 *Kulturtörténeti szemelvények a Nádasdyak 1540–1550 es számadásaiból (Texts for the Study of the History of Civilization, Selected from the Accounts Books of the Nádasdy Family for the Years 1540–1550)*, vol. II, Budapest, 1959, pp. 11, 14, 31, 36, 196; Kanizsa (1563), OL, *U. et C.*, 101:19; Munkács (1570), *M. Gt. Sz.*, 1896, p. 79; Kapuvár (1584), OL, *U. et C.*, 56:33, etc.

66 For example, *aratra sex cum bobis arabilibus 48, item bigis, iugis, vomeribus et omnibus instrumentis ad ea attinentibus, quibus exercuerunt allodiaturam additis mercenariis idoneis pretio conductis* (Szendrö (1570); but refers back to the middle of the century).

67 OL, *Documents municipaux et caméraux*, Fol. Lat. 913.

68 *Kulturtörténeti szemelvények. . . , vol. II, pp. 20, 25.

69 Kanizsa (1564), *M. Gt. Sz.*, p. 68; Esztergom (1580), Acsady, op.cit.,

pp. 125, 142; Cegléd (1584), *M. Gt. Sz.*, 1898, p. 345; Tihany (1588), *ibid.*, 1905, pp. 199–200, etc.

70 To take one example, the land register of Vöröskö (1543), which illustrates the same period. In it references are made to the need to employ, quite apart from the corvee, paid labour for most of the work (ploughing, harvest, threshing, gathering of crops, wine-growing, reaping). Anything 'outside custom' must be paid, it states. *Urbáre feudálnych panstiev na Slovensku*, vol. I, pp. 10, 152–5. The decree of Munkács (1570) requires the steward to have the estate vineyards cultivated '*partim subditorum gratuita opera, partim vere mercede operariis conductis*' (*M. Gt. Sz.*, 1896, p. 68).

71 For the land register of Gyula, see *Archives of the Town of Gyula*, pp. 87–90; for that of Világosvár: OL, Dl., 37 000; the information on Esztergom is given by Fügedi, *Századok*, 1960, nos. 1–3, pp. 97–8.

72 For the land register of Hédervár, see *Héderváryoklt*, vol. II, pp. 185–6. The information on Komárom in *M. Gt. Sz.*, 1897, pp. 492 (cf. OL, *U. et C.*, 4:45); the rest in the published texts quoted, *Urbáriumok, XVI–XVII. század*.

73 See, for example, H. Sée, *Histoire économique de la France*, vol. I, Paris, 1948, pp. 125 et seq.; M. Bloch, *Les Caractères originaux de l'histoire rurale française*, new edition, Paris, 1960, vol. I, pp. 105 et seq.; J. Meuvret, 'Domaines ou ensembles territoriaux? Quelques exemples de l'implication du régime de la propriété et de la structure sociale dans la France du XVIIe et du XVIIIe siècle', in *Première Conférence Internationale d'Histoire Économique*, Stockholm, 1960 (ed. F. Braudel, M. M. Postan, E. Söderlund), Paris-The Hague, 1960, pp. 343 et seq.; G. Duby, *L'économie rurale et la vie des campagnes dans l'occident médiéval*, Paris, 1962, vol. II, pp. 599 et seq.

74 See, for example, R. H. Tawney, 'The rise of the gentry 1558–1640', *Economic History Review*, 1940; E. Lipson, *The Economic History of England*, vol. I, 9th edn, London, 1947, pp. 133 et seq.; H. R. Trevor-Roper, 'The gentry, 1540–1640', *Economic History Review*, 1953, Supplement 1; L. Stone, 'The Nobility in Business, 1540–1640', in *The Entrepreneur*; Papers presented at the Annual Conference of the Economic History Society at Cambridge, England, April 1957, pp. 14–21; J. Cornwall, 'The Early Tudor Gentry', *Economic History Review*, 1965.

75 Quoted by Takats, op.cit. (*Poor Hungarians*), p. 143.

76 *Bornemissza Péter válogatott írásai* (*Selected Writings of Péter Bornemissza*), *1553–1584*, Budapest, 1955, p. 229.

77 Cf., for example, H. Mottek, *Wirtschaftsgeschichte Deutschlands*, vol. I, Berlin, 1957, pp. 333 et seq.; F. Luetge, *Geschichte der deutschen Agrarverfassung vom frühen Mittelalter bis zum 19. Jahrhundert*, Stuttgart, 1963, pp. 101 et seq.; W. Rusinski, 'Hauptprobleme der Fronwirtschaft im XVI. bis zum XVIII. Jahrhundert in Polen und den Nachbarländern', *Première Conférence Internationale d'Histoire Économique*, Stockholm, 1960, pp. 418

et seq.; J. Valka, 'La structure économique de la seigneurie tchèque au XVIᵉ siècle', *Deuxième Conférence Internationale d'Histoire Économique*, Aix-en-Provence, 1962, Paris-The Hague, 1965, pp. 211 et seq.

78 Cf. Z. P. Pach, 'Über einige Probleme der Gutswirtschaft in Ungarn in der ersten Hälfte des XVII. Jahrhunderts', *Deuxième Conférence Internationale d'Histoire Économique*, Aix-en-Provence, 1962, pp. 223 et seq.

Nine

History and Climate

Emmanuel Le Roy Ladurie

Until the eighteenth century when societies were still essentially agricultural and dominated by the never-ending problem of food supplies, there was an intimate link, which is now a thing of the past, between history and climate. Unfortunately these traditional societies have left us almost no sustained quantitative or homogeneous records of temperature and rainfall. Because of this lack of any first-hand written records the discussion of meteorological fluctuations and their effects on economic history has frequently been ill founded and very much confused. This article is therefore very much concerned with methodology; its aim is not to establish any complete solution, but rather to suggest avenues of approach.

Hampered by the shortage of data, research workers dealing with the question were quite often reduced to collating, entirely at random, events which had for various reasons caught the imagination of contemporaries: 'terrible' droughts, periods of 'dreadful' cold, 'hard' winters, 'torrents' of rain, floods. We can well imagine the subjective, heterogeneous, piecemeal, in a word, irrelevant, character of such material. One swallow does not make a summer: nor does a series of catastrophic frosts within the space of a few years *a priori* constitute a 'cold period'.

Such meteorologico-historical research was thus generally founded more on robust faith than on factual information, which in any case was scarce and unconvincing.

It was in this spirit that Bruckner boldly explained the fall of the Roman Empire by a deviation in the cyclone route and the drying-up of the Mediterranean region. Underlying all such work was the unsupported and very doubtful assumption that the fundamental determining influence on history is that of climate.

Interesting and well informed though it is, the work of the Scandinavian historian, Gustav Utterström, 'Climatic Fluctuations and Population Problems in Early Modern History',[1] is not free from the double weakness of anecdotal method and climatological assumption. The article in question assembles almost all the available data on the influence of climate on medieval and modern history; in a way it represents one of the extremes reached by the traditional method, and it will therefore be useful to analyse it here at some length before considering other methods.

The author is at pains to prove the existence of long periods of climatic deterioration, the effects of which he considers to have been disastrous for the European economy; basically the argument covers the fourteenth, fifteenth and seventeenth centuries.

He states that there was a general trend towards a colder climate in the fourteenth and fifteenth centuries. In support of this initial assertion Gustav Utterström presents numerous but quite heterogeneous facts. The first is that between 1300 and 1350 cultivation of cereals no longer occupied the most important place in the economy of Iceland; it gave way to fishing. We may regard this as a somewhat ambiguous event which might be given an economic interpretation just as much as a climatological one. But the chronology of the polar region is brought in to support the climatological interpretation; the advance of the glaciers, which began 'around 1200', affected Iceland in the fourteenth and fifteenth centuries, 'continued' in the sixteenth, and reached its maximum in the seventeenth and eighteenth centuries. The advance of the polar region is said to be confirmed and dated by the collapse of the Norman colonies in Greenland in the fourteenth century. This collapse was brought about by the subtle combination of the advance of the 'inlandsis' and its unexpected consequence, the advent of icebergs and the mass arrival of Eskimos in pursuit of seals.

The decline of English viticulture in the fourteenth century, after reaching a peak in the thirteenth, is given as further evidence. This, too, is explained as a consequence of the climatic revolution and is no longer seen as a straightforward symptom of economic regression. Was it not, moreover, that same peak in English wine production in the twelfth and thirteenth centuries which induced a British meteorologist to assert boldly that English summers in the twelfth and thirteenth centuries were hotter than in the present age? ... True, German wine-growing did not decline to the same extent after 1300–50; but the author says it is an established fact that apart from a few short periods there were only 'occasional' good years for wine in Germany in the fourteenth and fifteenth centuries; by such means is further evidence provided of the general deterioration in climatic conditions.

In the view of the Scandinavian historian, the later fifteenth century (after 1460) and the first half of the sixteenth century had the advantage of having a far milder climate than the previous period; there followed another period of increasing cold and hardship around 1560 which continued into the seventeenth century. What is the evidence? In Sweden cereal production is said to have 'dropped' between 1554 and 1640; we should indeed very much like to know how variations in 'cereal production' in Scandinavia in the sixteenth and seventeenth centuries have been measured. But let us not dwell on the matter; we learn that at that time the south-west Baltic and the Thames, which had not frozen between 1460 and 1550, once again experienced severe winters in the second half of the sixteenth century and the first half of the seventeenth century. In England, cherry orchards spread towards the north of the country about the beginning of the sixteenth century, but in the reign of Elizabeth a 'cooler' climate once more prevailed. Finally, the advance of the glaciers sets in again at the end of the sixteenth century and in the seventeenth century. This is the period of the 'little ice age'. The peak of this advance of the polar region, 'the most considerable of the post-ice age', was reached in the Alps and in Iceland in the middle of the seventeenth century.[2] There followed various ups and downs, but no marked recession was felt until after about 1890.

In support of this theory, the author also mentions the period 1596–1603, the years immediately preceding and following 1630, the 1649–52 and 1675–7 periods and the 1690s, which were all disastrous to the Scandinavian economy.

The arrival of Baltic cereals in the Mediterranean from the 1590s onwards and the depopulation of Spain in the seventeenth century are also put forward by Mr Utterström as obvious symptoms of climatic change, as is the fall in the number of sheep in Spain after 1560 and especially after 1600.

In short, the seventeenth-century crisis, which is of such great historical importance, also has climatic origins; the author says it is vain to try to explain it solely in terms of the internal European economy and the society of the age.

In all, this constitutes a rich and varied harvest of facts and data. But certain facts seem to us to be open to criticism. In the first place, we must stress once again that a large number of these are not *a priori* of a climatic nature (decline of wine-growing or sheep-rearing, spread of wheat or cherries, still less any radical change in cereal trade). According to our present knowledge of the matter they are explained just as well, if not better, in purely economic terms. However, when the author mentions certain years of climatic hardship and agricultural under-production in the fourteenth and seventeenth centuries, he is presenting us with truly meteorological data. But what he must do is show us, by means of rigorous, statistical methods, that these disastrous years resulted from more or less corresponding meteorological conditions; and having done so, he must show that they occurred with exceptional frequency during the long period under consideration, and that they were more or less unknown, or at all events considerably less frequent, in the preceding and ensuing periods. As long as no proof has been given of any significant difference between any two periods, we cannot accept the disastrous years in question as units in a long series, and we are forced to see them as forming only part of short-term meteorological fluctuations. Assuming that he is following a reliable method, is the author entitled to incorporate these facts in his argument, the object of which is to distinguish long-term climatological fluctuations? What should we say of a historian or of an economist that claimed to show a lasting, long-term rise in prices if he based his argument on a few peaks in the curve he professed to interpret, and neglected or did not even know its general path? Should we not accuse him of trying to prove a long-term movement by making undue use of data and evidence that refer only to the short-term? By the same reasoning, we shall see that a few remarkably cold winters scattered about the seventeenth century do not, without ampler information, amount to a 'cold seventeenth century'.

Of the evidence used by G. Utterström, only the ice data really indicate long-term climatic movements; but the chronology of these long-term movements is too imprecise, their real extent and significance too uncertain for us to be able to draw from them alone conclusions as ambitious as the ones suggested by the author. What should we say of a historian who undertook to explain the whole of Europe's economic progress since 1850 in terms of the retreat of the glaciers, well known to have taken place in the Alps and more or less everywhere from 1850 onwards? But would it be any more unjustified than postulating, as Mr Utterström does, a close connection between the advance of the glaciers and the economic crises in Europe in the fourteenth, fifteenth and seventeenth centuries?

It thus appears that research must look for new paths to find an escape from the impasse into which traditional methods have led it. It must turn to methods of climatological study, biological or at least historico-statistical methods, which, ruling out any pre-conceived ideas from the start, and being essentially positive, aim in the first instance at establishing rigorous annual series of meteorological data, which are continuous, quantitative and homogeneous. Once this preliminary step has been taken and the climatic factor isolated and identified, the historian can proceed to try to determine the possible influence of this factor on the life of men; all he knows for the time being of this influence on traditional societies is the vague fact that it was never totally determining, but that it was not negligible either.

The first and most highly developed biological method is dendro-climatology;[3] the basic concept is well known: any cross-section of a tree-trunk reveals a series of concentric rings; each ring represents the annual growth of the tree, and the number of rings gives the tree's age.

However, whereas all the rings in a given tree thus have an obvious chronological value, each ring taken separately has its own climatological value; it reflects history, the history of the favourable or unfavourable meteorological conditions prevailing in the year in which it was formed. A favourable year is represented by a wide, thick ring, an unfavourable year by a narrow line, sometimes hardly discernible. The tree ring fully integrates the meteorological data for the year in which it grew. It supplies a sort of climatic note on the year in question. If we draw a graph with the sequence of years as the x-axis and the thickness of the rings as the y-axis, we obtain the 'growth curve' of the tree, a curve whose fluctuations, correctly interpreted, reveal yearly meteorological fluctuations.[4]

But a question arises here: what do we mean by 'favourable or unfavourable meteorological conditions'? And first of all, what are the determining conditions, i.e. temperature and rainfall? Reason and experience give the same answer: everything depends on the location.

In a semi-arid country—North Africa or the south-western United

States, for example—where there is a chronic lack of rain, while the tree is scarcely ever lacking in warmth during the vegetative period, any long series of generally very narrow rings at once denotes a marked period of drought; conversely, a succession of thick rings indicates a humid period.

In regions near the polar circle—in Scandinavia or Alaska, for instance —the temperature is a critical factor and one can safely say that a narrow ring represents a particularly cold year; a thick ring represents a milder one.[5]

In temperate zones—western Europe or New England, for example —tree growth depends at one and the same time on temperature and rainfall, and the interpretation of growth curves is made more difficult through the combination of different factors.

So it is not entirely by chance that dendroclimatology has in the first instance developed in marginal climatic regions where the interpretation of curves is unambiguous and direct; the regions most widely prospected by the specialists are in fact Scandinavia and Alaska on the one hand, and the semi-arid south-west of the United States on the other (Colorado, California and Arizona). The University of Arizona has, through the work of A. E. Douglass, now continued by Edmund Schulman, obtained some very interesting results in this field.[6]

From Douglass in the first decade of the twentieth century came the decisive impulse for the growth of the new discipline. The presence in the western United States of trees and groups of trees—conifers of all types, particularly sequoias, whose age varied between 500 and 1,500 years—considerably stimulated research. One of the initial aims of the work was archaeological: having established from living trees a rigorous chronology of specially dry and humid years from the fourteenth century onwards, Douglass was able to identify on the beams of Indian *pueblos* the characteristic pattern of a certain number of these remarkable years. Establishing thus in which century the tree which the Indians had used to make the beam had lived, and determining the year in which it had been felled, by means of the growth ring next to the bark he was able to give the exact date of the *pueblo* in which these beams had been employed, either for construction or maintenance purposes. This method, replaced nowadays by dating techniques based on the life of radio-active bodies (carbon 14), had made it possible to give the exact chronology of a considerable number of Indian *pueblos*.

But Douglass also saw all the importance of such work for the study of the history of climate: and his work, continued today by his pupils,

Growth figures for trees in North America 15th-20th centuries

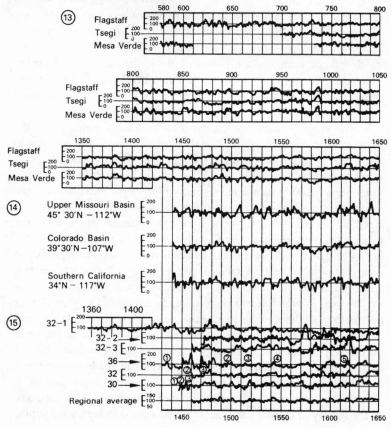

Figure 13 Average growth of trees in the south-west of the United States (15th–20th centuries).

Comparison of divergence from the average width of growth rings for two localities in North Arizona and for Mesa Verde in south-west Colorado. Data obtained from living trees are completed in upper river areas by series of figures taken from archaeological beams.

Figure 14 Drought and rainfall in the western United States (15th–20th centuries).

Figures for regional growth, obtained from trees which are sensitive to drought, correspond to the major and even the secondary fluctuations in the flow of nearby rivers and thus show themselves to be good pluviometric guides for earlier centuries.

Figure 15 Tree growth in the Mackenzie delta in Canada (15th–20th centuries). 32–1, 32–2 and 32–3 are based on individual trees; 36, 32 and 30 on groups of three. The numbers in circles represent the number of trees covered for each curve. The regional average is composed of five groups of trees, two of which have not been individually shown here.

Sources: (Fig. 13) E. Schulman, 'Tree Ring Indices of Rainfall, Temperature and River Flow'.

(Fig. 14) E. Schulman, 'Tree Ring and History in the Western United States'.

(Fig. 15) G. L. Giddings, 'Mackenzie River Delta Chronology'.

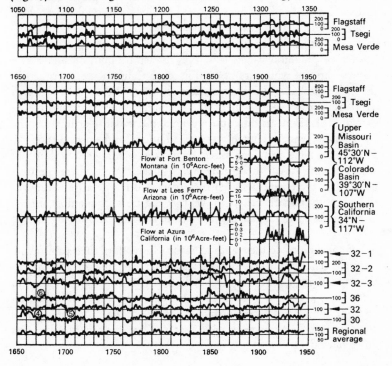

has made it possible to achieve some remarkable results in this field, of which Figs. 13 and 14 show the final and, as it were, the overall results.

For the three curves in Fig. 13, periods of time—more than a thousand years altogether—are shown on the x-axis and the relative thickness of growth rings on the y-axis: in composing these three curves, Schulman made use of data from three groups of conifers which are very sensitive to drought. Of these three groups of trees which are far more than one hundred years old, some even attaining one thousand years, two are situated in the north of Arizona, at Flagstaff and at Tsegi respectively; the third is situated in south-west Colorado, at Mesa Verde. At Mesa Verde and at Tsegi, the conifers used are *Douglas* firs; at Flagstaff, a variety of pines. Each of the three curves, we should note, has great representative value, since it involves an average derived not from one tree, but from a group dispersed throughout one of the three regions mentioned. Individual changes in the life of each tree (diseases, etc.) are thus compensated for, and all that is shown is the general tendency of regional climate: at a higher level, the agreement of the three curves, which can easily be established from the graph, enables us to form a picture of the general trend in climate throughout a whole geographical area (Fig. 14).

Fig. 14 has less historical value since it begins only in 1440, but it has greater geographical value: its curves in fact are built on nine forest groups, three of which are situated in south California, three others in the Colorado basin, the other three in the upper Missouri basin; in all 51 trees were covered—all of them conifers especially sensitive to drought. These curves thus give a general picture of the climate of the whole of the western United States. In addition, for the period 1900–50, E. Schulman has provided three curves representing the volume of water flowing down the nearby rivers in the region where the trees grew. The agreement between these data and the data from the tree rings is truly remarkable. It shows that the trees in question are excellent measures of rainfall, that they are in fact natural rain-gauges.

What conclusions do these authors reach as a result of their painstaking research? The first is that climate was generally stable during the last thousand years and in fact during the last two thousand; 'beams cut 1,700 years ago show growth rings which are identical with those of trees of the same species growing today on the same sites'. This conclusion is in agreement with that reached by other authors on different evidence.[7]

But a second conclusion, which is far more interesting for the historian, concerns the occurrence of fairly broad meteorological fluctuations which here concern rainfall. During periods lasting as long as twenty or thirty years and sometimes even a whole century, the curve shows a marked variation from the average path and enables us to recognize waves expressing long periods of drought or humidity. The most marked of these fluctuations is situated around 1300: 'We have a very clear impression,' writes E. Schulman, 'after studying very old conifers, that a century of very great drought in the south-west was followed from about 1300 by an almost uninterrupted century of rainy years. This very wet period was perhaps the longest in the region throughout the last two thousand years.' The curves derived not from living trees but from the beams of Indian *pueblos* tend to confirm this view.

It is thus shown that in the western United States the thirteenth century was dry and the fourteenth humid. Was this fluctuation in climate restricted to America, or did it include Europe? It will be impossible to answer this question until similar studies have been undertaken in the same systematic way on the old continent.

This distinct oscillation of rainfall, affecting two entire centuries, was, by reason of its length and intensity, the most marked of all those recorded by the pines and firs of North America in the last thousand years. Far behind it, but of all the main fluctuations second in size, comes the long drought in America at the end of the sixteenth century: 'the last 25 or 30 years of the sixteenth century in the south-west', Schulman writes, 'were generally characterized by a severe deficiency in tree-growth, rainfall and river-flow, far more marked than in the famous droughts of 1900 and 1934; the data provided by very old trees tend, in fact, to show that it was the worst drought ever known since the century-long drought starting around 1200.' Schulman also notes important regional differences in distribution of this drought; very severe in California, where it lasted from 1571 to 1597 and where the rain deficiency, as recorded in the reduced growth-rate of trees, was almost twice as severe as any other comparable deficiency recorded between 1450 and 1950; very intense too in Colorado, where it can be dated exactly between 1573 and 1593; far less pronounced in the north, in Oregon, where it is revealed only by a slight intermittent deficiency in the growth of trees between 1565 and 1599.

Geographical differentiation of this kind is important in itself and is of a general character; it is quite wrong to apply conclusions valid for arid zones categorically to humid, temperate regions; what is true for Los Angeles is not necessarily true for Portland; in Europe what may be true for the Mediterranean is not necessarily true for countries on the North Sea, still less for the Baltic.

However that may be, this long and severe drought at the end of the sixteenth century certainly had major consequences in the region where it was most severely felt, the south-west of what is now the United States: it was, Schulman tells us, far severer than the major droughts of the twentieth century in the same region, those of 1900 and 1934. None the less, these two had disastrous effects, if we can go by John Steinbeck's two novels devoted to them: *To a God Unknown* (the 1900 drought) and *The Grapes of Wrath* (that of 1934). The great drought of the end of the sixteenth century certainly had even more devastating effects on the backward and scattered economy of the Indians who, grouped in their *pueblos*, engaged in irrigation agriculture in Arizona, Colorado and New Mexico.[8] It is also probable that it had a depressive effect on the new colonial economy of the nearby Mexican plateau. The Matlazahualt epidemic (1576–9) and the accompanying economic depression, whose negative effects on Atlantic trade[9] have been pointed out by Pierre Chaunu, may well be related to this large-scale meteorological fluctuation, and the latter may be integrated in this way into general economic history.

The counterpart of all this work on rainfall, carried out in arid zones, is the historical work carried out on temperature in Arctic regions. Here the thickness of the ring is proportionate to the total heat received during the growth period. Giddings[10] has thus been able to reconstruct five centuries of climatic history in the Arctic region (1450–1945) on the basis of groups of trees situated near the Mackenzie river delta (north of the Arctic Circle, near the frontier between Canada and Alaska). Here too, the essential finding is the general stability of the curve, which oscillates throughout the centuries around one and the same average, and rises only slightly from 1850 onwards[11] (Fig. 15).

We have some difficulty in finding, on this extremely accurate curve, those long-term periods of cold which, according to Gustav Utterström, were responsible for the major periods of economic depression. On the other hand, decimal and even smaller fluctuations in temperature can easily be discerned on this graph: one of the most prominent is the series of hot summers between 1628 and 1650. There is little doubt that similar fluctuations, which cannot, it is clear, be synchronized with

American fluctuations, had devastating or beneficial effects in Europe, especially in northern countries and mountainous regions, depending on their upward or downward direction. This field too is still untouched in Europe.

All in all, this dendroclimatological work seems to us to present a twofold interest. First, from the methodological point of view: the rigorous chronology, the strict annual, continuous nature of the curves, the use of local and regional averages and their inter-comparison, the use of trees and zones particularly sensitive to certain climatic factors, all contrast with the uneasiness we feel in reading traditional works on the history of climate, based on disjointed, scattered, disparate and sometimes insignificant data.

But there is also a certain degree of directly historical interest: true, nothing authorizes us to conclude from American meteorology that there was a similar meteorology in Europe: Schulman has strongly opposed the so-called 'teleconnection' attempts made by the Swede, E. de Geer. He had claimed that he could date beams from a Scandinavian fortress by placing their characteristic ring series on a reference scale taken . . . from Californian sequoias: an attempt clearly doomed to failure! One meteorology cannot be deduced from another when the width of a continent and an ocean separates them; American trees cannot do the work of European trees. However, they can provide us with assumptions and supply useful hypotheses on certain aspects of our own climatic history: for example, the absence of any significant long-term fluctuation in the growth of trees in the United States and Canada between 1450 and 1850 leads us to doubt not the existence of the little ice age (for it is more or less an established fact), but the real extent and influence of that phenomenon. If the biological evidence for the modern period in Europe is as unrevealing and devoid of long-term fluctuations as in America, we shall be forced to admit that the little ice age was only a prolonged but weak climatic oscillation, without any importance for the life of men.

Conversely, the proved existence of long-term oscillations in climate in the American West about 1300 stands as a fairly plausible argument on behalf of Mr Utterström's thesis concerning the existence of similar oscillations in Europe in the same period; this does not in any sense mean that the Scandinavian historian's idea is thus confirmed. On the contrary, everything still remains to be proved. In this respect all we can say is that the existence of a long humid period in America in the fourteenth century, the generally verified existence of an advance of the polar region in Iceland and Greenland and of a very high level of the Caspian Sea during the same period,[12] suggest the possibility of a long period of adverse climatic conditions in the fourteenth century. It would still remain to be seen to what extent this phase, if it really took place, helped to imperil an economic and demographic balance which, in any case, had already become extremely precarious by reason of the progressive crowding together throughout previous centuries of our population 'which had become too dense in relation to food production';[13] we should for instance ask ourselves whether such a climatic period, besides aggravating economic and social conditions which were in themselves unfavourable, might not have contributed to the onset and aggravation of the great pandemic diseases of the fourteenth century, either directly through action on pathogenic germs, or, more likely, indirectly via subsistence difficulties and physiological distress resulting from adverse agricultural conditions which, themselves, were born of climatic misfortune . . . this seems to me to be the problem. As to a solution, there will not be one until the day that systematic studies similar to the American ones throw light on European climatology in the thirteenth, fourteenth and fifteenth centuries, and at the moment, such studies are totally lacking.

The American trees provide us with assumptions and working hypotheses in respect of long-term movements in climate in Europe, but nothing more. On the other hand we are already certain of one thing in respect of short-term movements: the systematic study of very old trees carried out in Scotland[14] for the sixteenth and seventeenth centuries has revealed not a long-term oscillation, but approximately ten-year cycles of groups of summers which are in the main either cool or warm. These are the same types of cycles which have already been observed in America; they are similar, though not synchronous. Once a large number of studies of this kind have been completed, knowledge of these cycles will probably throw new light on agricultural, and thus on economic, history. But even then we should not naïvely assume the effects of any given meteorological conditions, for instance the alternation of wet and dry cycles, on crops. In Mediterranean regions, a series of very dry years is catastrophic; in the northern part of France, on the other hand, it is often a rainy summer that is disastrous. Gaston Roupnel[15] has shown this clearly for Burgundy in the years 1640–50, and his work is confirmed by the experience of 1957 and 1958. The effects of prolonged rain are to beat standing crops flat, then to cause the sheaves to rot in the field and the grain to germinate; the most promising crop may be largely lost because of humidity, when it has not been dried and gathered in time.

One last point: data taken from trees would be of even greater interest if they revealed not only the empirical succession of meteorological cycles, but also a law governing regularity by which we could predict the return of such cycles and know their frequency, and thus bring into history and planning a truly rational element.

A certain journalist has, it is true, on the basis of the long-standing work done by Douglass and Antevs, thought it possible to assert that dendroclimatology established the influence on climate of the 11·4-year sun spots. The temporary disappearance of the ten-yearly cycle from growth-ring curves between 1645 and 1715 led even Douglass to suppose that the reign of Louis XIV had been marked by a veritable dearth of sun spots. And the same journalist was able to write for all readers with a taste for the sensational: 'the trees were right: we know that by a curious decision of fate, the reign of the Sun King was marked by the almost total absence of spots on the surface of the star of light.'[16]

In fact, those who have continued the work of Douglass are far more cautious than their master on this controversial topic. Commenting on the assertions of Douglass, Edmund Schulman writes: 'Certain examples of direct parallelism that have been noted between the solar cycle and the growth of certain trees are often referred to and, in fact, may not be entirely due to chance.' And having made this extremely sober general statement, he tells us what he is actually thinking: 'Cycles observed in the growth of trees seem to be characterized by variation in length, extent and form, and tend to appear and disappear without any general principle emerging, and they tend to take place in almost any order. No satisfactory physical explanation of these characteristics has yet been provided.'[17]

We must therefore stop expecting growth-curves of trees to supply us with information about a universal law on the cyclical evolution of climate. Just as with price curves, climatic curves are for the time being purely empirical: it is impossible to deduce them on the basis of a given frequency; they must be established for each individual continent, and for each large region.[18]

Pending the establishment for Europe of reliable 'dendroclimatological' theories, which would require much time and extensive resources, there is a simpler and quicker method that enables us to form a picture of west European climate since the sixteenth century. This method, which has been known for three-quarters of a century in France, is based on the study and knowledge of the fructification dates of plants.

It is the so-called 'phenological'[19] method. The principle here is very simple: the date of ripening of fruit depends essentially on the temperatures to which the plant is subject between formation of the buds and its final fruiting. The warmer and sunnier this period is, the quicker and earlier is maturity—and therefore the harvest, if we are dealing with a cultivated plant. Conversely, if the months of growth have been cold, cloudy and dull, maturity and the harvest will be late. For a great number of plants, there is a close correlation, which has been shown accurately between the sum of temperatures for the growth-period and the dates of flowering and fructification; these dates thus serve as precise climatological guides.

For the historian, this field of research is a very limited one: the *ancien régime* has left us hardly any material on the annual dates of flowering of lilac and roses. . . . There is, however, one date which is faithfully recorded every year in many municipal records: that of the grape harvest, where the latter is made the object of a proclamation. The date, fixed by experts appointed by the town or village community, obviously depends upon the maturity of the grape and thus constitutes a good guide to the average meteorology of the growth-period in any given year, from March–April to September–October. 'Les raisins sont assez meurs et mesmes par endroits se seichent' ('the grapes are quite ripe and are even drying in places'), in the words of the experts, 'juges de la maturité du raisin' ('judges of the ripeness of the grape'), and the nine elders appointed by the municipality of Montpellier on 25 September 1674. And thus they fixed the grape harvest 'a demain' ('for tomorrow') and the first cuvée 'contée de judy prochain 27 du courant . . . unanimement conclu'[20] ('reckoned from Thursday next, the 27th of the present month . . . unanimously agreed'). 'Les raisins sont à maturité (the grapes are ripe), in the words of the experts of Lunel[21] on 12 September 1718, who fixed the grape harvest for 19 September, and their opinion is in line with those expressed throughout the wine-growing areas of Europe—for the grape harvest that year, 1718, from Languedoc to the Black Forest, was particularly early.

Of course, economic and social factors join these purely climatic factors affecting the proclamation of the wine harvest. In Burgundy, at the beginning of the nineteenth century, the owners of better quality wines, generally well-off and able to take risks, endeavoured to obtain quality and preferred late harvests. The owners of ordinary vines were not much worried about the quality of their wine and tried to make the harvest as early as possible.[22] In addition, the time of maturity of the grape varied according to the type of vine. In spite of these 'interference' factors, Garnier has managed to show that there is excellent agreement, if not perfect correlation, between the phenological curve for the wine harvests of Argenteuil, Dijon and Volnay in the nineteenth century and the average temperatures from April to September for the corresponding years as recorded at the Paris Observatory (Fig. 16).

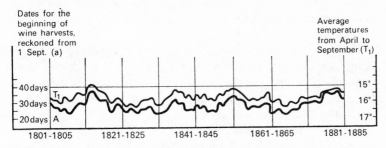

Figure 16 Dates of wine harvests and temperatures (mobile five-yearly averages). [N.B. To enable a comparison with the phenological curve A to be made, the temperature curve T_1 has been inverted.]
Source: W. M. Garnier, 'Contribution de la phénologie à l'étude des variations climatiques'.

Fig. 16 enables us to establish the following principle: early wine harvests, warm year; late wine harvests, cold year, or, more exactly, cold growth-period.[23] We can easily see the great importance of the wine harvest dates in the periods for which we have no continuous series of temperature records, and in particular for the seventeenth century in Europe, the climatology of which is so controversial, precisely because so little is known about it.

Almost the only source for such dates of wine harvests is Angot's great article which assembled the results of a national survey (one might even say a European survey) carried out by the central meteorological office of France about 1883: a great number of viticultural research establishments provided Angot with abundant information on the eighteenth and nineteenth centuries. For the seventeenth century and the end of the sixteenth, Dijon, Salins and Kürnbach (Black Forest), Lausanne, Lavaux and Aubonne (Switzerland) gave figures for the dates of wine harvests which have almost no gaps at all. The figures for Dijon, Salins and Lausanne go back to the beginning of the sixteenth century, but have some gaps. Those for Dijon go back to the fourteenth century. In brief: phenological data are extremely abundant for the nineteenth century, very ample for the eighteenth, adequate for the seventeenth, but too sparse before that.

At the end of his enquiry, Angot concluded—as the American dendroclimatologists of today have done—that there had been stability in the French and the west European climate from the sixteenth century to the present day. However, as he was simply a meteorologist and not a historian, he was only interested in the idea of stability and did not study fluctuations for themselves: we should now like to draw attention to these same fluctuations (Fig. 17).

Fig. 17, which we constructed on the basis of the data published by Angot, shows on the y-axis the dates of wine harvests reckoned from 1 September in a certain number of towns or districts, all situated between the Alps, the Black Forest and the Massif Central; the x-axis gives the year (from 1600–1800).

The first thing we note is the excellent, if not complete, annual agreement between these various curves; the year 1675 clearly shows this, where the wine harvest was everywhere unusually late in the whole of Europe, from the Black Forest to Languedoc. The summer that year was in fact very cold, and Madame de Sévigné writes to her daughter, who at that time was in Provence: 'Il fait un froid horrible, nous nous chauffons et vous aussi, ce qui est une bien plus grande merveille' (28 June 1675) ('It is terribly cold, we have to have the fires lit and you do as well, which is an even greater wonder'); on 3 July the Marquise once more noted 'un froid étrange' ('a strange coldness'); at the height of summer, on 24 July 1675, she writes again: 'Vous avez donc toujours votre bise. Ah! ma fille, qu'elle est ennuyeuse!' ('So you've still got your cold wind. Ah! my dear, what a nuisance!') and then she wondered 'si le procédé du soleil et des saisons était changé'[24] ('whether the pattern of the sun and seasons had changed'). Similarly the year 1725 which was marked by continuous mists and rain throughout the summer, and by a tremendous rise in the price of grain, most of which rotted while still standing in the fields, is also remarkable for the universal lateness of the wine harvest. Conversely, the year 1718, when spring[25] and summer[26] were very dry and hot, when the springs and wells dried up, when there was no hay in the whole of the Languedoc, is shown on Fig. 16 by its wine harvests, which were everywhere very early. The same is true for the year 1636, which was a year of very great drought,[27] and the year 1645, which was a fine hot year, a year of excellent wine, of 'vin furieux' ('heady wine').[28]

Agreement seems equally good among our various districts for short-term cycles, between two or three years and ten or fifteen years.[29] Series of years (or more precisely growth-periods) that were particularly warm can easily be discerned on our graphs: 1635–9; 1680–6; 1704–10;[30] 1718–19 (two of the hottest and driest summers in the eighteenth century); 1726–8; 1757–62, and finally 1777–85. The latter years, which were particularly hot and dry, were accompanied by over-production and a consequent slump in the prices of wines and grain, which should be related to the pre-revolutionary economic crisis. Conversely, we should observe the cold growth-periods: the graph confirms the fact that between 1639 and 1643 and again between 1646 and 1650, France experienced a series of cold, wet summers which proved disastrous to grain production. Taking purely traditional material as his basis, Roupnel also notes: 'After 1646 on the other hand, we meet with a succession of wet years, icy springs and stormy summers which every-where destroyed the already inadequate crops of this depopulated and ruined region [Burgundy].' This confirms the phenological curve. He adds a general reflection: 'It would indeed be interesting to determine the nature of these wet periods. In the seventeenth century, excess rainfall is caused, so it seems, by summer rain, that is by storms in June and July. At present, fodder plants benefit from heavy rainfall and a rainy year often brings prosperity to the grower. For the vine, it is always a disaster. But in Burgundy in the seventeenth century, a dry year was more welcomed by our ancestors than by us today. On the other hand, a rainy year, with its storms and hail, often brought destruction of the cereal crops, which at that time were the essential product and practically the sole source of food supplies.'[31] He does not hesitate to write in addition: 'Six rainy years from 1646 to 1652 resulted in a terrible state of affairs in the spring of 1652.'

True, it would be absurd to 'explain' the Fronde in terms of the unfavourable meteorological conditions of the 1640s. On the other hand, it is reasonable to suppose that in a society that was in a state of latent crisis 'since 1630, 1635, 1637', agricultural difficulties, which were born of adverse climatic conditions, played a contributory role; bad harvests caused 'the extraordinary cyclical peaks' of 1647–50. They did not, in the deepest sense of the term, cause the tremendous 'eco-nomic, social and above all, democratic upheaval' which was partially

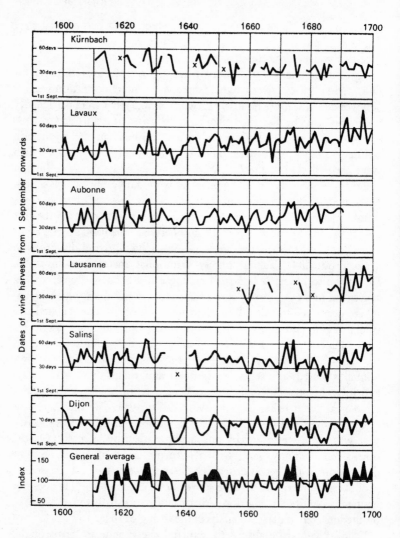

Figure 17 Wine harvests in the 17th and 18th centuries. Price of wheat per measure (*setier*) according to E. Labrousse.

The curves and the general average have been built on Angot's figures. Some of the dates for which we have no information have, wherever possible, been filled in by making use of corresponding curves taken from neighbouring areas. To facilitate comparison with fluctuations in other branches of agriculture, we have shown, at the foot of the table, the wheat price-curve for the 18th century, as drawn up by Labrousse (*Esquisse*, p. 98).

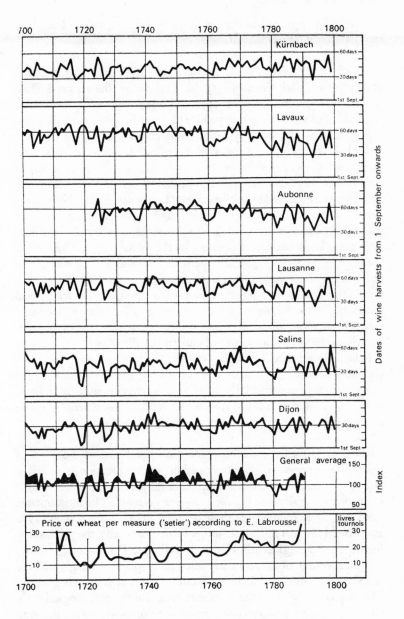

Dates of wine harvests from 1 September onwards

and clumsily expressed in the revolutions of the Fronde,[32] but like a catalyst, they did precipitate it.

After two very violent peaks in 1673, and especially 1675, we find practically no 'black series' of very cold years before the very end of the seventeenth century, between 1687 and 1704. The wine harvests of 1692 and 1698 were nearly everywhere the latest between 1675 and 1725; and in that same decade, at Salins, as at Dijon, there were no early wine harvests comparable with those of 1684, 1686 or 1718. The disastrous effect of the winter of 1693 on the European economy is already common knowledge.[33] It is probably less well known that all the 1690s were marked by prolonged heat deficiency during the growth-period, a deficiency which, in Baltic countries—the main countries supplying cereals—must have slowed down, hampered and sometimes even completely prevented ripening of the 'bleds' (corn). Thus might we explain, at least in part, the persistent difficulties encountered in obtaining grain supplies, especially in the countries of the north[34] during this period, as well as the high price of grain, and the widespread food riots in the whole of Europe and even as far away as Siberia,[35] throughout these years: riots and difficulties which cannot be adequately explained by the winter of 1693 and by the wars.[36]

Following a period of respite (1704–10), a new series of cold years occurred between 1710 and 1717: all in all, the period 1687–1717 seems to have been particularly ill favoured by climate, since, in addition to the two long series of cold years which we have just described, it also suffered the two catastrophic winters of 1693 and 1709.

Chance has, to a large extent, made the second part of the reign of Louis XIV a period of climatic hardship: such a situation is probably not entirely unconnected with subsistence difficulties and the economic stagnation generally termed 'the end-of-reign crisis'. The most notable 'cold periods' to follow were those between 1740 and 1752, round 1770 and from 1785 to 1789. Here, too, a comparison with the price-curve for wheat in the eighteenth century, according to E. Labrousse,[37] shows that these cold periods were fairly often accompanied by high prices of cereals and subsistence difficulties. From 1765 onwards these beginnings of a correlation between the economic cycle and the phenological cycle take the form of a fairly close parallel development; waves showing high prices and low prices, over-production and insufficiency of crops coincide fairly precisely with the series of cold years around 1770 and the warm years around 1780. This probably has to do with the fact, which is very clearly brought out on our curve, that for 1770 and 1780 these meteorological cycles were far more consistent, far more marked and decisive than similar cycles in the preceding period in the eighteenth century and they therefore must have had a far more serious influence on agricultural economy. Cereal production in the Massif Central, for instance, was seriously affected by these cold years: between 1767 and 1773, there is practically no wheat at all from Causse on the market of Montauban.[38] Conversely, the viticultural over-production crisis of 1777–85 was aggravated by the series of mild springs and hot and dry summers shown on our graph.

So far the conclusions to be drawn from west European phenology correspond with those of west American dendroclimatology, at least for the period following the sixteenth century: primacy of decennial fluctuations (the most notable being the 1687–1704 cold period); fairly probable existence of inter-decennial fluctuations, of which the most marked may be grouped as follows (see Fig. 17—general average):

Overall Series of Springs and Summers

Hot	Cool
1651–1687	1687–1717
1717–1739	1739–1758

On the inter-decennial level a link with agricultural conjunctures and thus with general conjunctures is probable, particularly in the reign of Louis XIV; for wheat produced in Brie and for rye produced in the regions of the north, 1687 is a decisive turning-point: Jean Meuvret[39] has clearly shown that a period of low prices and relative over-production of cereals, which had started at the latest in 1661, was succeeded from 1685–90 by a long period of hardship and high prices lasting until about 1715: cooler springs and summers made for scarcer and dearer cereals. Let us finally note the total absence from our graphs of any regularity in these cycles: is there in fact any need to say that the solar cycle[40] has no influence on phenological curves?

Over and above short and average fluctuations on which the phenological method gives us some valuable information, is it possible from 1550–1600 onwards to identify long-term fluctuations, or any long-term movement in climate? This is a question of capital importance for the study of the economic history of this period.

In fact a superficial view of any phenological curve might lead us to think that the existence of such movements was detectable: thus, the wine harvests at Lavaux became later and later between 1640 and 1710; in the first half of the seventeenth century the wine harvest at Lavaux took place between 20 September and 10 October; in the eighteenth century, far later: the grapes were gathered between 10 and 30 October.

This is a truly magnificent example, it will be thought, of the progressive cooling-down that began during the reign of Louis XIV. But how then are we to explain the fact that this delay in the grape harvest appears at Dijon fifty years later? As for Salins and Kürnbach, the average date of the grape harvest hardly varied at all in the seventeenth and early eighteenth century; if there was any change, it was rather in the other direction, i.e. towards an earlier harvest. Did the vineyards in Franche-Comté and Germany differ in climatic conditions from those in Switzerland and Burgundy? Obviously not. The close agreement between short- and average-term phenological cycles from widely separated vineyards shows clearly that the weather is the single predominating factor which synchronizes the harvest times of village communities as far apart as Germany and the South of France. Conversely, an obvious divergence in long-term movements, particularly between vineyards very near one another, cannot result from climate. The progressive lateness of the wine harvests, at Lavaux or at Dijon for example, is due to human action. The reason is known: at times in the seventeenth and eighteenth centuries, vine-growers, stimulated by a strengthened but more discriminating demand, ceased making the traditional inferior product in order to produce a better wine with better keeping-qualities;[41] in Guyenne and Languedoc they distilled their wine to make eau-de-vie from it. In both cases they had good cause to delay the harvest: by doing so they obtained a grape which was riper, with a higher sugar content, capable of giving a higher '*degré*' ('more strength'). The extreme limit was the '*pourriture noble*'. Such practices shifted the whole phenological curve upwards. This was a sign of a revolution in wine-growing, not in climate, and the delay of the grape harvest in fact reveals a most interesting piece of economic history; for this lateness in wine harvests to have any meteorological significance and to indicate a long-term climatic change, it would have had to take place in all vineyards at the same time. We have in fact seen that this was not so. Thus, the biological guide does not indicate any long-term fluctuation in meteorology in the seventeenth and eighteenth centuries superimposed on the short and average cycles, which are perfectly clear and synchronized on all the graphs. We may also say that if any prolonged wave of this kind did take place, it remains unimportant for the historian, since its biological consequences, the only ones which would count, were imperceptible. Although certain other authors have felt that there were long-term climatic oscillations, these are essentially ones affecting the winter period (which has no influence on the phenology of the grape); we will discuss their arguments below.

Thus the ancient vineyards of Germany, France and Switzerland echo, far-off but in harmony, the evidence of the thousand-year-old forests of Alaska or Arizona: in the modern period, after 1500, 'plant documentation' shows countless short- and average-term fluctuations but no long-term change: 'the seventeenth century had weather no worse than the eighteenth.'[42]

In other words, the great crises of the seventeenth century, that of the Fronde, and that of the years between 1690 and 1700, were probably produced by successions of climatically and ecologically unfavourable years; knowledge of the phenological data will probably make a vital contribution to the study of these basic phenomena and of the agricultural crises that preceded the French Revolution. On the other hand, 'the seventeenth-century crisis', in the broadest sense of the term, i.e. the prolonged depression, the long-term unfavourable conjuncture, during which these sharp short-term crises occurred, cannot possibly be explained in terms of climate, which as far as the growth-period is concerned was the same we may be sure as in the sixteenth[43] and eighteenth centuries.

In the explanation of a long-term economic movement covering a whole century, the history of economic and social conditions, i.e. proper human history, thus regains its supremacy, overshadowing climatological factors and their limited cycles.[44]

These latter factors seem to us to be truly and especially important for economic history considered on an annual, decennial or even on an inter-decennial scale; on a long-term scale, they cancel each other out. The short-term is their domain; the long-term is beyond them, at least after 1500 in the period for which we have data.

The detailed information which biological methods provide is incomplete on one essential point: the factors are seasonal, they concern solely the months in which sapwood and the grape develop (spring-summer); they say nothing of the winter, the period in which there is a total halt in growth and temporary suspension of plant life in temperate regions. This is probably one of the essential reasons for the disagreement with ice chronology, where winter fluctuations certainly play a major role.

Owing to the lack of biological sources for the study of winters, we are indeed obliged to resort to the episodic documentary method mentioned and criticized at the beginning of this article. In its rough and purely qualitative form this method, as we have seen, must be treated with the greatest reserve. On the other hand, if used carefully and rigorously, it can provide interesting results. An English meteorologist, D. J. Schove,[45] has thus drawn from the anecdotal hotchpotch of traditional written works a systematic and chronological census of winters which, since 1450, have been reputedly 'cold' or 'mild' and of summers said to be 'warm' or 'cool'[46] in north-west Europe. Basing his work on about ten regional series thus established, he has built up decennial averages, which themselves have been transformed into mobile thirty-year averages (1501–30, 1511–40, 1521–50, etc.). He has thus refined, improved and transcended the 'anecdotal' method by drawing up statistics, and he has managed to some extent to move from the qualitative to the quantitative plane. We should note that D. J. Schove systematically excludes any ambiguous data. He makes use only of strictly meteorological facts; his arguments are rigorous and firmly based. His conclusions thus merit our interest; we set them forth here, though we do not always adopt them in our own arguments; but we regard them as useful working hypotheses.

The conclusions, when we deal with the winters' climate, are very different from those suggested by summer data, and the table which our author has drawn up for the climate of the sixteenth century makes this clear (table 1). The summer series on it show fluctuations that attain and sometimes exceed twenty years, but there is no long-term temperature fluctuation. In other words, in decennial periods there are varying numbers of warm or cool summers; but over the sixteenth century as a whole these variations compensate one another, and simply leave us with an impression of general stability. Episodic sources thus rigorously exploited fall perfectly in line as far as the summer is concerned with the conclusions independently drawn from phenological data.

It is quite another matter with winters; data from Italy, Basel, Flanders and other European regions (summaries are given in table 1) prove that from the 1540s onwards, the number of mild winters decreases suddenly, while the number of severe winters rises sharply and clearly, and this process continues until at least 1600.

Thus from 1540 onwards, against a relative constancy of summers, and the absence of any summer trend, we have a steady worsening of winters. More than the advance of the glaciers, more than the actual cooling of winter months, it is their relative cooling-off in relation to the summer, the widening gap between increasingly divergent seasons, which, according to D. J. Schove, constitutes the essential manifestation of the 'continentalization' of climate and the onset of the 'little ice age'. According to him the worsening of winters or the continental tendency in fact persisted long after the sixteenth century (table 2), and in spite of marked fluctuations (in particular an 'inter-glacial' period of mild winters between 1681 and 1740), it only ended, and perhaps not finally, in about 1890. The turning-point of the 1890s, which was spectacularly marked by the retreat of the glaciers, which has been continuous since then, is according to Manley (another English meteorologist quoted by D. J. Schove), 'a change in winter temperatures, in conjunction with a strengthening of the "maritime" element in European climate'. Finally it is said that this turning-point denotes the end of the 'little ice age', or at least a new inter-glacial period. The two great turning-points in winter climate in Europe are thus said to be 1540 and 1890.

At first sight, we are somewhat surprised and even a little sceptical, in the face of this fundamental disagreement in scale between series for summers, with their relatively short fluctuations and long-term stability, and series for winters, subject to broad long-term oscillations, and even inter-secular ones. At all events we should like D. J. Schove to publish his detailed evidence for the period 1600–1950, as he has done in perfectly convincing fashion for the period from 1500–1600. The table in which he sums up his work (table 2), although extremely fertile in suggestions, is only a summary, based on data supplied by thirty-year mobile averages; publication of the averages themselves, in other words the basic data for the table, would enable us to assess the evidence and speak with greater confidence.

There is no doubt that the general hypothesis of D. J. Schove concerning the 'little ice age' would, if it were fully proved, be extremely fruitful. It would in fact clear up the very disturbing contradiction, which so far has been irreconcilable, between biological information showing climatic stability, and information based on the glaciers, showing long-term climatic pulsations. Or, more precisely, it would show that this contradiction derives not from the inadequacy of research, but from the facts themselves and the difference between the seasons; winter (i.e. glacial) fluctuations, on this hypothesis, being on a completely different scale from summer fluctuations (the latter being revealed by biological data).

In any case, the concept of the 'little ice age', as held by our author, is vague, since, looked at closely (table 2), this 'age' turns out to be a series of shorter oscillations of about 50 to 100 years, causing series of generally cold winters to alternate with periods of respite, when there are frequent milder winters. Has there in fact been, as D. J. Schove would have us believe, a predominance of cold periods, and thus an accumulation of them constituting an 'age' covering several centuries? Could we not just as truly say that, by and large, warm and cold periods compensate each other? And that, in that case, it is unwarranted to speak of long-term climatic change? More detailed evidence and better statistical analysis will no doubt enable us to resolve the question.

We must add that it is the refinement of D. J. Schove's analysis, as much as the range of his conclusions, that commands our attention.

Even taken at a more modest level, the idea put forward by D. J. Schove of a disagreement, a permanent discrepancy, between winter and summer fluctuations, is indeed of very great interest from a methodological point of view. Thanks to this concept and the chronological analyses which it prompts, we are able to move away from the narrow and one-sided notions suggested by biological methods—'hot growth-period' or 'cool summer'—to arrive at developed, complex notions which are more truly historical: as the seasons diverge, as a more sharply marked gap appears in some periods between harsh winters and scorching summers; or, on the other hand, as the seasons come to resemble each other in a monotone of mild winters and cool summers, we may speak, not so much of a 'warmer' or 'colder' climate, which means little, but of a 'more continental' trend or a 'more maritime' trend in the weather.

In our author's view, the first half of the sixteenth century was a maritime period, which can be fairly well compared with the first half of the twentieth century. Maritime conditions reached a peak in the 1520s, 'when winters were extremely mild, and summers cool,[47] and the weather generally extremely humid'. The Seine and the Tiber reached levels during that period which have not been equalled since. Prophecies all speak of the coming flood. 'An ark was in fact built in the South of France, and the mud in the regions surrounding the Danube was so terrible that H. G. Wells, writing about the Turks at Vienna (1529), says that they were beaten rather by the weather than by the defenders of the town.'

On the other hand, the following period is said to have shown a continental trend: after the 1540s, 'hotter summers[48] (until about 1560) and the colder winters (at least until the end of the century) suggested a complete change, with a weakening of West-East movement and an increase in the frequency of East winds', in other words a continental-ization of climate.

Although this continental tendency remains on the whole the dominant one for D. J. Schove until the end of the nineteenth century, the maritime element is more prominent at times: for example, between 1681 and 1740, a period of mild winters, termed 'inter-glacial'. Pheno-logical data, apparently unknown to D. J. Schove, confirmed these periods and defined them more exactly: thus the series of very cool summers represented by the late wine harvests of 1687–1717 is the counterpart of the generally mild[49] winters which the English author indicates for the same period. It thus appears that the second half of the reign of Louis XIV was a perfectly typical period of maritime climate. Conversely, the preceding generation between 1651 and 1680 ex-perienced 'very cold' winters (table 2), but also, with few exceptions (1673, 1675), early wine harvests, indicating generally warm summers (Fig. 17). Continental climatic conditions, i.e. a marked difference between winter and summer, were thus present throughout the year during these thirty years and the first part of the reign of Louis XIV well deserves the description 'very continental' given it in table 2.

Let us here end these analyses which, with inadequate data, it is impossible to carry further.

If the 'little ice age', or, to speak more soberly, the large-scale series of cold winters, and the trends towards a 'continental' climate are an undeniable fact ('overwhelming', in the words of D. J. Schove) from 1540 onwards, what were the specific effects of this trend towards continental conditions on agricultural economy, and on the production of basic foodstuffs?

The usual view, mentioned at the beginning of this article, is that the effects were in general catastrophic. It is difficult to accept these assertions; the starting-date of the 'little ice age', 1540, does not in any way correspond to the turning-point in the economic 'conjuncture'[50] or in the demographic situation, which was at that time in the middle of a period of expansion. The turning-point comes much later, at the end of the sixteenth century, or even at the time of the Fronde.

Conversely, the seventeenth-century crisis, which has sometimes been put forward as the human and historical outcome of the 'little ice age', in fact reached its most violent phases in periods of climatic abatement during which the maritime influence temporarily prevailed over the continental influence (1630s, Fronde, 1690s).

What is more, if 'continentalization' had the adverse effects on agriculture which it is said to have had, the first part of the reign of Louis XIV, which until about 1681–5 had a clearly continental climate, would have been marked by subsistence difficulties, in contrast to the second part. But we know that the very opposite is true: the low prices and relatively plentiful supply of foodstuffs for the period 1661–85 contrast sharply with the more or less constantly rising prices and general hardship marking the later phase (1687–1717). And, as we have seen, this can be quite easily explained: maritime periods, with their misty and cool summers, can in the long run be more unfavourable to cereal production than continental periods, with hard winters but summers that are often very sunny. A cold winter furthermore is not really injurious to agriculture unless it follows a few weeks of mild weather which have deprived the earth of its protective covering of snow and allowed growth to start (1709, 1956, for example); only in such instances, which really are exceptional, is it catastrophic. In other cases, a cold winter in no way harms cereal crops. We must add that by definition it has no influence at all on spring-sown cereals (whose economic importance increases as one approaches the north of Europe), which are sensitive only to spring and summer hazards.

Let us sum up: it cannot be shown that continentalization had a depressive effect on the agricultural economy of Europe. The mere fact that it was operative in economic periods as different as the sixteenth, seventeenth and eighteenth centuries, not to mention the nineteenth, suffices to make this point clear.

We must not go from one extreme to another, and, because we have cast doubt on the harmful effects of a long-term 'continental' trend, conclude that it benefited agriculture. True, the question is open, but at the present stage in work it cannot be answered: the partial analogies which we felt we might propose between phenological curves and parallel economic curves are not possible in this new sector, which is far more complex and less familiar. First, the most precise chronology for 'continental' periods, that established by D. J. Schove (table 2), is based on thirty-year mobile averages, and is therefore not rigorous enough to allow any comprehensive comparison with economic chronology, which nowadays is established in an infinitely more precise way. Second, whereas phenology gave evidence of a relatively simple phenomenon, warmth or coolness of the spring and summer period, a phenomenon which in certain conditions is capable of exercising a specific influence on crops, 'continentalization' is a complex phenomenon; it depends on a contrast between colder winters and generally hotter summers, a contrast which is capable, depending on the variable 'dose' of these two seasonal elements, of exercising an active influence on agriculture, with contradictory results varying from one year to the next.

In that case, no conclusion is possible on this particular point for the time being. Progress in historical and agricultural meteorology will probably enable us one day to see clearly into this matter and determine with relative precision the actual effects of large-scale fluctuations of the continental or maritime type on agriculture and economic life.

To complete this record of our uncertainty, we should add that the fundamental causes of the 'little ice age', or the successive continental fluctuations which have been grouped under this convenient title, are almost unknown. True, we know their immediate causes: weakening or partial deviations of the constant flow of Atlantic depressions that pass from west to east towards the European coast, and the predominance on our continent of anticyclones, chiefly in winter. But why are these depressions diverted—are the causes terrestrial or cosmic? We ask in vain. The good old sun spots have been brought in here; but the attempt is vain: 'the sun spots and aurora borealis curve drawn up by Brooks is quite distinct from the ice curve.' With notable detachment, Schove mentions other cosmic hypotheses: 'recent observations of the fact that circulation of the red spot on Jupiter (a body hovering in the atmosphere of Jupiter and carried round by the planet's movement) varied in the same way as the flow from the west on the Earth, leads us to think that there may be some variation in the sun's ultra-violet light, and perhaps the "little ice age" may in the last analysis be explained, as Hoyle suggested with regard to the great ice ages, as the effect of varying amounts of spare matter in interstellar space.' But the historian, who is even less qualified than the meteorologist, can treat such hypotheses, which so far have been more or less unsupported, only as objects of a kind of poetic curiosity. Let us return to the earth: 'for the time being all that we can do is to gather and synthesize the biological and historical facts, in order to establish a clear and chronological picture of the climatic changes which have really taken place.'[51]

All in all, the facts mentioned above are both less interesting for the present and richer in content than phenological data: less interesting for the present because, being too complex, they provide us with less clear and less firm correlations with agricultural and economic phenomena. But they are richer perhaps because of their very complexity: they suggest the possibility of integrating phenological data into a composite and much more complete picture of climatic history, and by this very fact obtaining a deeper knowledge of history.

All these conclusions, at least as far as European climate is concerned, are obviously only of a provisional nature and must be subject to revision in the light of new facts. Certain methodological observations, however, seem to us to be incontestable, and we here sum them up. Of the four methods we have described, the first (traditional anecdotal method) is to be rejected; the second (dendroclimatological method) is perfectly scientific, but slow, delicate, laborious and costly, and hardly within the scope of the individual researcher. On the other hand the last two methods mentioned are both easily handled and of undoubted value; they offer the additional advantage of being exactly complementary. It is therefore in that direction that we should organize research, towards the knowledge of growth-periods and, to a certain extent, of agricultural fluctuations, by means of phenology;[52] towards the study of the dead season and winter fluctuations by establishing statistics on the basis of records; and thus towards a comprehensive knowledge of the history of climate by the parallel study, or if one prefers, the contrasted study of the two series, winter and summer, thus established.

Such series, for the period from 1500 to 1800,[53] are entirely accessible. They have an intrinsic value. They are also valuable, not to say necessary, for the building-up of a complete and true history: the description of meteorological fluctuations as they really took place will, in fact, once and for all overthrow that empty form of determinism which gratuitously attached a climatic explanation to every large-scale economic or demographic event that could not easily be otherwise explained. But it will also make it possible to establish the true role of climate in the history of traditional societies, a role which is neither a leading one nor a minor one; it will make it possible to determine the extent to which chance and the contingency of seasons and harvests have conspired with, opposed and sometimes diverted the profound trends and the imperious demands of historical development.

Finally it will give a new colouring, a truly tangible quality to economic and social history.

Notes

1 *Scandinavian Economic History Review*, vol. III, no. 1, 1955. The article gives a very full and helpful bibliography of recent articles on the history of climate.

2 The seventeenth-century ice peak was also noted in the Caucasus.

3 For dendroclimatology, see two series of publications: pre-war publications, A. E. Douglass, *Climatic Cycles and Tree Growth*, Carnegie Institute of Washington, Publ. no. 289, 3 vols, 1919, 1928, 1936; Anteus, *The Big Tree as a Climatic Measure*, Carnegie Institute of Washington, Publ. no. 352; idem, *Rainfall and Tree Growth in the Great Basin*, Carnegie Institute of Washington, Publ. no. 469; W. S. Glock, *Principles and Methods of Tree Ring Analysis*, Carnegie Institute of Washington, Publ. no. 486.
Post-war publications, which deal with the whole question anew, and on which our article is founded: the entire series of the *Tree Ring Bulletin* published by the University of Arizona and two fundamental articles by Edmund Schulman, 'Tree Ring and History in the Western United States', *Smithsonian Report for 1955*, pp. 459–73, Smithsonian Institute of Washington, 1956, and 'Tree Ring Indices of Rainfall, Temperature and River Flow', *Compendium of Meteorology*, American Meteorological Society, Boston, 1951. See also J. L. Giddings, 'Mackenzie River Delta Chronology', *Tree Ring Bulletin*, April 1947.
European works based on the above do not take the most recent developments in dendroclimatology into account and devote a lot of space to the actually very doubtful correlation between tree-growth cycles and solar cycles: F. E. Zeuner, *Dating the Past, Introduction to Geochronology*, London, Methuen, 1949 (ch. I); A. Laming, *Découverte du passé*, Paris, 1952; A. Ducrocq, *La Science à la découverte du passé*, Paris, Amiot-Dumont, 1955.

4 It is impossible to give a complete survey in this article of all the methods used by dendroclimatologists; let us simply point out that as the average thickness of rings diminishes outwards from the centre (youth—vigorous growth) towards the periphery of the tree (old age), not only the actual thickness of each ring is taken into account but the difference between the actual thickness and the average thickness the ring should have in relation to its distance from the centre.

5 'Cold year' here implies 'cold vegetative period'.

6 The American school, moreover, had illustrious precursors: Leonardo da Vinci, Buffon, Duhamel du Monceau and Candolle, each in turn considered tackling the 'dendroclimatological' problem. Cf. R. A. Studhalter, 'Early History of crossdating', *Tree Ring Bulletin*, April 1956.

7 V. M. Garnier, 'Contribution de la phénologie à l'étude des variations climatiques', *La Météorologie*, Oct.-Dec. 1955.

8 R. Mousnier, *Les XVIᵉ et XVIIᵉ Siècles*, Paris, P.U.F., p. 934.

9 Pierre Chaunu, 'La grande dépression du Mexique colonial', *Annales*, 1957, no. 3, p. 514.

10 Giddings, op. cit.

11 This rise can probably be connected with the slight increase in warmth implied by the general retreat of the glaciers in the world from the same date; but Giddings does not give any opinion on this matter.

12 According to Gustav Utterström, op.cit.

13 E. Perroy, *Le moyen Âge* (*Histoire générale des Civilisations*, Paris, P.U.F.), p. 406.

14 Schove, 'Tree Rings and Summer Temperature A.D. 1501-1930', *Scottish Geographical Magazine*, June 1950, quoted by Gustav Utterström, op.cit.

15 *La ville et la campagne au XVIIᵉ siècle. Étude sur les populations du pays dijonnais*, Paris, S.E.V.P.E.N., 1957, p. 33.

16 A. Ducrocq: article in *Science et Avenir*, Dec. 1955, and *La Science à la découverte du passé*, op.cit.

17 Schulman, 'Tree Ring and History', op.cit., p. 473, and 'Tree Ring Indices', op.cit., p. 1028.

18 B. Huber and W. von Jazewitsch, 'Tree Ring studies', *Tree Ring Bulletin*, April 1956, p. 29.

19 On phenology, cf. the fundamental article by A. Angot, 'Étude sur les vendanges en France', *Annales du Bureau Centrale météorologique en France*, 1883. See also Garnier, 'Contribution de la phénologie' and J. Sanson, 'Températures de la biosphère et dates de floraison des végétaux', *La Météorologie*, Oct.-Dec. 1954, pp. 453-6; Duchaussoy's 'Les bans de vendage de la région parisienne', ibid., March-April 1934. Convincing examples of the phenological method in A. A. Lindzey and J. E. Newman, 'Use of official data in spring time, temperature Analysis of Indiana phenological Record', *Ecology*, vol. 37, no. 4, Oct. 1956 (contains a very good proof of the close correlation between the temperature and dates of flowering of a great number of plants). On the practical applications of phenology in agriculture, see Golzov, Maximov and Iaroschevski, *Praktische Agrarmeteorologie*, Berlin, Deutscher Bauernverlag, 1955 (translated from the Russian).

20 Archives Municipales de Montpellier, H H 20.

21 Archives Municipales de Lunel, B B 21.

22 R. Laurent, *Les Vignerons de la Côte d'Or au XIXe siècle*, Dijon, 1958, ch. III.

23 This concept is especially valid for northern wine-growing regions: in the French Midi, lack of rain would also have its effect alongside temperature in fixing the date of ripening of the grape. In this work we have therefore made use only of series of wine harvests in northern regions.

24 *Lettres de Mme de Sévigné*, Paris, Hachette, 1862, vol. III, pp. 499, 506, 523.

25 Note by a priest: 'depuis le dernier jour de Mars, nous n'avons pas veu de pluye et nos fontaines sont bien basses . . . les ollives et les raizins sont presque tous séchés et les ollives tombées des arbres' ('since the last day of March, we have had no rain and our wells are very low . . . the olives and grapes have almost all dried up and the olives have fallen from the trees'). (Aniane, Arch. Municip. AA 2, vol. 67, 25 Aug. 1718.)

26 'Les chaleurs furent extrêmes cette année-là ; elles durèrent tout le mois de juillet et d'août et ce ne fut qu'au sixième de septembre qu'on commença d'avoir de la pluye qui rafraîchit toute la campagne' ('The heat was extreme that year; it lasted the whole month of July and August and it was not until 6 September that we started to get some rain, which refreshed the whole countryside'). (D'Aigrefeuille, *Histoire de Montpellier*, vol. II.)

27 J. Sanson, 'Y a-t-il une périodicité dans la météorologie?' *La Météorologie*, 1955.

28 Roupnel, op.cit., p. 33, quoting the diary of Father Macheret.

29 J. Garnier, a meteorological engineer, thus defines the cycles on the phenological curve: 'Les variations des vendanges se font tantôt dans le sens de la précocité, tantôt dans celui de la tardivité' ('Variations in the dates of the wine harvest sometimes show an early tendency, sometimes a late tendency'). He adds that we find 'des périodes plus tardives et plus précoces correspondant aux périodes sèches et chaudes ou aux périodes humides et froides' ('later and earlier periods corresponding to dry hot periods or wet cold periods').(J. Garnier, op.cit., p. 299.)

30 In spite of the winter of 1709, which was outside the growth period; in general phenology gives no information whatsoever on the period of rest of oceanic and continental plants, i.e. the winter.

31 G. Roupnel, *La ville et la campagne au XVIIe siècle*. . . , p. 33. Peasant sayings confirm Roupnel's ideas: 'Année pluvieuse, année malheureuse' ('wet year, wretched year'); and, similarly, 'Année de foin, année de rien' ('year of hay, year of nought'). Conversely, 'Année sèche n'amène jamais famine' ('a dry year will never make you starve'); 'Année sèche n'appauvrit pas le maître' ('a dry year won't make the master poor'); 'Année sèche n'est pas affamée' ('a dry year isn't a hungry year'); 'Année sèche, année de vin' ('a dry year is a year of wine') (given by J. Sanson, 'En marge météorologique de la petite histoire', *La Météorologie*, June 1956).

32 The quotations are taken from P. Goubert, 'Ernst Kossmann et l'énigme de Fronde', *Annales*, 1958, no. 1, p. 117.

33 P. Goubert, 'Problèmes démographiques en Beauvaisis', *Annales*, 1952, no. 4, p. 461. J. Meuvret, 'Les crises de subsistances et la démographie de la France d'Ancien Régime', *Population*, Oct.-Dec. 1946.

34 J. Meuvret, 'Les mouvements des prix, de 1661 à 1715, et leurs répercussions', *Bulletin Soc. statistique de Paris*, May-June 1944.

35 R. Portal, 'Russes en Sibérie au XVIIe siècle', *Revue d'Histoire moderne*, June 1958.

36 Using other methods, Manley has also reached the conclusion that a cold period took place between 1691 and 1702; Manley, 'Variation in the mean temperature of Britain since glacial time', *Geologische Rundschau*, 1952, pp. 125-7, given in G. Utterström, op.cit.

37 E. Labrousse, *Esquisse du mouvement des prix et des revenus au XVIIIe siècle*, Paris, Dalloz, 1933, p. 98.

38 'The largest number of years in which there was a complete failure of wheat from Causse (9 months out of 12) 1739-89, are spread over a period of 5 years between 1767 and 1771. We can deduce from this that meteorological conditions were not favourable to wheat production' (Robert Ancely, 'Le prix des Céréales à Montauban (1691-1789)', Diplôme d'Études Supérieures (unpublished)).

39 J. Meuvret, 'Les mouvements des prix'.

40 Cf. Angot, op.cit.

41 Cf. H. Enjalbert, 'Naissance des grands crus', *Annales*, Oct.-Dec. 1953, p. 462.

42 E. Labrousse, *La Crise économique à la veille de la révolution*, Paris, P.U.F., 1944, p. 182, n. 1.

43 The incomplete series of grape harvests for which we have figures in the sixteenth century show no overall climatic difference with the seventeenth century, at Dijon, Salins and Lausanne.

44 We once more make an exception for the 14th century where a long-term fluctuation in climate, although it has not been shown yet, is not inconceivable.

45 D. J. Schove, 'Discussion: post-glacial climatic change', *Quarterly Journal of the Royal Meteorological Society*, April 1949; refer to this for tables 1 and 2, often quoted in our article, but which could not be reproduced here.

46 We should state that such a statistical attempt seems to us to be superfluous in respect of summer, for which the phenological information seems to be sufficient. On the other hand, for winter, statistical attempts have enabled us to draw up an irreplaceable 'catalogue'.

47 The coolness of summers in the 1520s is confirmed by the figures for wine harvests during this period, which are, unfortunately, all too rare and full of gaps. At Salins, Dijon and Lausanne the wine harvests on which we have information were late during this decade. At Salins, the wine harvests of 1527, 1528 and 1529 took place at the end of October, a record which is

broken only during a few rare years in the seventeenth and eighteenth centuries (Angot, op.cit.). These data do not seem to be known to D. J. Schove, whose ideas they very happily confirm.

48 In fact the wine harvests of the 1550s were, generally speaking, early: the standing record is beaten in 1556 and 1559 at Dijon where the wine harvest took place at the end of August (Angot, op.cit.).

49 If D. J. Schove's description is right, the winters of 1693 and 1709 were thus exceptions.

50 Except on the monetary plane, which is nothing to do with the question being dealt with here.

51 Conclusion of D. J. Schove's article.

52 We should note here another advantage of phenology over dendroclimatology: a tree ring is simply the sort of biological evidence of the yearly experience undergone by a single biological individual. Several dozen trees are needed to compose a valid average. On the other hand, the date of a wine harvest already makes an average assessment of the ripeness of the grape over several thousand examples (or tens of thousands) of vines; in itself it possesses statistical value.

53 After 1800 such series would have no value; they are dispensed with by temperature and rainfall records. Before 1500, it would seem very difficult to draw up 'phenological' series, owing to lack of material. The example of Dijon (where the series starts at the end of the 14th century) shows nevertheless that such material may exist.

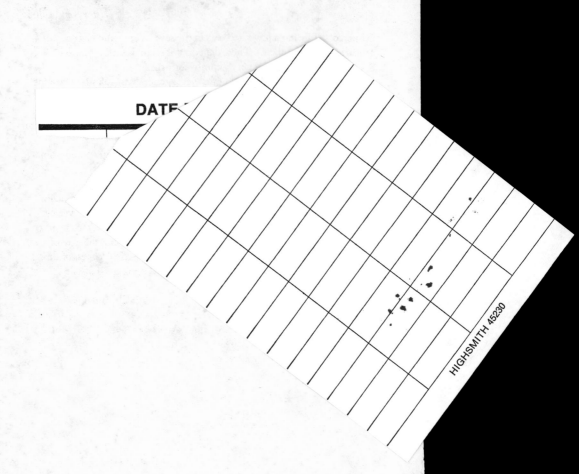

DATE

HIGHSMITH 45230

72 73 74   12 11 10 9 8 7 6 5 4 3 2 1